D1489487

MODERN WORLD NATIONS

Finland

Douglas A. Phillips

Series Editor
Charles F. Gritzner
South Dakota State University

An imprint of Infobase Publishing

Dedication

This book is dedicated with love to seven key women in my life: my grand-mother, Rena Hook; my mother, Carolyn Phillips; my wife, Marlene Phillips; my daughter, Angela Phillips Burnett; my sisters, Cheryl Burroughs and Betsy Jones; and my cousin, Lauree Benson. The key to their strength is their faith, which has served as an inspiration to those they touch.

Frontispiece: Flag of Finland

Cover: Market Square in Helsinki, Finland

Finland

Copyright © 2008 by Infobase Publishing

Chelsea House
An imprint of Infobase Publishing
132 West 31st Street
New York NY 10001

Library of Congress Cataloging-in-Publication Data
Phillips, Douglas A.
  Finland / Douglas A. Phillips.
    p. cm.— (Modern world nations)
  Includes bibliographical references and index.
  ISBN-13: 978-0-7910-9671-0 (hardcover)
  ISBN-10: 0-7910-9671-8 (hardcover)
  1. Finland—Juvenile literature. 2. Finland—Social life and customs—Juvenile literature. 3. Finland—Civilization—Juvenile literature. I. Title. II. Series.

DL1012.P55 2008
948.97—dc22   2007040319

Chelsea House books are available at special discounts when purchased in bulk quantities for businesses, associations, institutions, or sales promotions. Please call our Special Sales Department in New York at (212) 967-8800 or (800) 322-8755.

You can find Chelsea House on the World Wide Web at http://www.chelseahouse.com

Series design by Takeshi Takahashi
Cover design by Jooyoung An

Printed in the United States of America

Bang NMSG 10 9 8 7 6 5 4 3 2 1

This book is printed on acid-free paper.

All links and Web addresses were checked and verified to be correct at the time of publication. Because of the dynamic nature of the Web, some addresses and links may have changed since publication and may no longer be valid.

Table of Contents

Finland

1

Welcome to the Land of the Finns

E xploring Finland is like finding a hidden treasure. Few know much about this far northern country or its people, the Finns. The average person's knowledge of Finland is minimal, and it often consists of a few facts: Helsinki is the capital; the country has Lapland; it is the Land of the Midnight Sun; and there are lots of reindeer. Actually, Helsinki *is* the country's capital; the country has more than 200,000 reindeer, most of which are in Lapland; and there is the long "midnight sun," which is matched by very long winter nights. There is so much more to know about the country and its people, however—an incredible tale of poverty to prosperity. Like the phoenix, a mythical bird that never dies and repeatedly rises from the ashes of tragedy, Finland and the resolute Finns have risen again and again and prevailed.

This book takes you on a journey that explores the geography of Finland, making many stops along the way to visit the country's landscapes and people. We will examine the physical, historical, political, social, economic, and other cultural aspects of Finland's geography in depth. It is an amazing story filled with conflicts, achievements, endurance, and ingenuity. At the same time, we will also look at the Finns and their future.

When a visitor meets a Finn, there is a warm welcome, but not too warm. The nature of these far northern people is somewhat reserved. The Finns are described as remote, serious, and with a no-nonsense approach in their straightforward relationships with others. Despite this, the Finns are also fun loving and enjoy the sauna, their national form of relaxation. Small talk doesn't usually last long, as Finns like to get to the point—unless they are in the sauna. The Finnish sauna is a place of retreat and an institution that you will visit in Chapter 5.

Finns have used their resolve to overcome many obstacles. First, they learned to live and prosper in a cold and challenging far northern environment. Later, intrusive neighbors frequently placed Finland at risk. During the past half century, Finns have carved out a niche in a world increasingly linked economically and by the flow of information. In all cases, the Finns were able to use their array of talents and their patience to rise again, like the proverbial phoenix, and prevail.

Finns call their country *Suomi*, which means "Lakeland" or "Swampland," and they refer to themselves as *Suomalaiset*. Finland's earlier stamps and coins used the word *Suomi*, but they have added the English term *Finland* in recent years. This book will use the common English term, Finland, and refer to the country's people as the Finns. A peoples' language and their ethnicity (self-identity as a people) often are the same. The primary language of the Finns is Finnish, but minor languages and ethnic groups represented in their country include Swedish, Russian, and Sami.

Finland is not a large country. It occupies an area of only 130,559 square miles (338,145 square kilometers), making it slightly smaller than Montana or Canada's Newfoundland

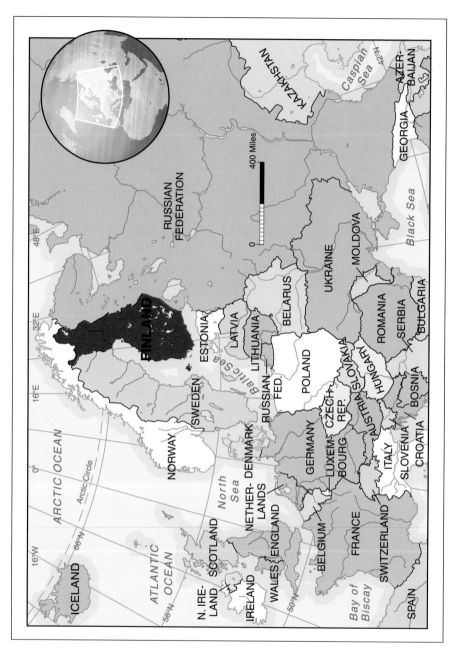

Finland is located in northern Europe and shares borders with Sweden to the west, Russia to the east, and Norway to the north. Estonia lies to its south across the Gulf of Finland. Covering an area of 130,559 square miles (338,145 square kilometers), the country is slightly smaller than Montana.

province. In the far north, in frigid and sparsely populated Lapland, the country shares borders with Norway, Sweden, and Russia. Its western border faces the Gulf of Bothnia. Sweden lies across this narrow northern extension of the Baltic Sea. The country's southern margin, which includes its capital and largest city, Helsinki, faces the Gulf of Finland. The country of Estonia is just a short ferry ride across this narrow eastward-extending arm of the Baltic. Finland's long eastern border faces Russia. Here, Karelia and other lands have long been contested between tiny Finland and its giant, often-threatening, neighbor.

Finland's population is also rather small, with a mid-2007 estimate of only 5,238,460 people. The country has fewer people than Arizona or Maryland, and slightly more than Toronto, Canada. The population density is about 40 people per square mile (15 per square kilometer), but this figure is quite misleading. Most Finns live in the warmer south where the bulk of the country's economic activity takes place.

The northern quarter of Finland is located at latitudes poleward (toward a pole of Earth) of the Arctic Circle, which slices across the country from east to west and also bisects the city of Rovaniemi. This city of more than 58,000 people is located in Lapland, and it is also the home of the internationally famous Santa Claus Village. Each year, youngsters from more than 150 countries write about 650,000 letters to Santa Claus. Finland's techno-savvy Santa even has a Web site and can be reached by e-mail. Here's the contact information for Santa's Post Office:

Tahtikuja 1
96930 Napapiiri
Tel. +358-(0)20 452 3120
Fax +358-(0)16–348 1418
joulupukinpaaposti@posti.fi
www.santaclaus.posti.fi

Santa Claus can be visited year-round in the city of Rovaniemi, in Santa Claus Village on the Arctic Circle. The village's attractions include a permanent Christmas exhibition, several souvenir shops and restaurants, and a post office. It is a popular destination for people from all over the world.

The Finns love their country and their lands. Their feelings are expressed in the following poem by Aleksis Kivi:

The Finnish Land

What is that land of hill and dale
That is so beautiful,
The land aglow with summer days,
Land with the northern lights ablaze,
Whose beauty all the seasons share,
What is that land so fair?

There many thousand lakes are bright
With twinkling stars at night
There many kanteles [stringed folk instruments] *resound*
And all around make hillsides sing
And on the golden heath first ring:
That is the Finnish land.

On this note, it is time to begin our exploration of Finland and its people. Although they are serious, the Finns also have a crazy sense of humor that pops up at unusual times. For example, they have developed new sporting events (discussed in Chapter 7) referred to as Finnwacky. In one event, participants see how far they can throw a mobile phone. In any case, whether serious or silly, the story of the Finns is a wonderful tale.

CHAPTER

2

Physical Landscapes

Just as musicians read notes and seek meaning in musical notation, geographers interpret maps. To a geographer, a well-crafted map can speak volumes. In a detailed map of Finland, several features provide clues to the country's past and present. For example, towns and cities are clustered in the southern part of the country, which serves as a reminder that much of the country lies in the frigid north. In fact, about a quarter of Finland reaches poleward of the Arctic Circle (66½ degrees north latitude). Finland lies at the same latitude as much of Alaska, the northern half of Hudson Bay, and southern Greenland. It is also impossible not to notice the thousands of lakes that dot the landscape as a legacy of the region's glacial history.

In the southern part of the country, a network of highways resembles a bicycle tire and spokes. Two roughly semicircular parallel highways form the tire: One closely hugs the coast, and the other is about 40 miles (65 kilometers) inland. The coastal highway accommodates settlements bordering the gulfs of Bothnia and Finland and attests to the importance of the sea to Finns. The second highway appears to enclose most of the country's lakes. To understand the significance of this location, you need only refer to the country's name, Suomi, or "swampland." The highway follows a terminal moraine, which is higher ground created when a huge glacier dumped its debris thousands of years ago. Highways that represent spokes of the wheel radiate outward from Jyvaskyla, Finland's fifth largest city, which is located near the center of the more densely populated southern part of the country. In this chapter, you will tour Finland's challenging physical conditions and resulting natural landscapes.

WEATHER AND CLIMATE

In order to understand much of Finland's physical geography, one must look to the very distant past. Land features, at least some of the natural vegetation, the region's soils, and its thousands of lakes and rivers all show the influence of continental glaciations. Huge sheets of glacial ice—some of it several miles thick—covered much of northwestern Europe during the Pleistocene epoch, or the ice age, as it is commonly called. These sheets expanded four times, only to retreat as conditions warmed. Today, Earth is once again in a warming period of glacial retreat called an interglacial. In essence, our planet has been warming for some 12,000 years, with a few short-term exceptions. In other words, conditions similar to the current global warming have occurred on numerous previous occasions, and they appear to result from natural fluctuations in such conditions as solar energy output, wobble of Earth's axis, changing ocean currents, and other factors.

Finland, one of the youngest nations in Europe, has thousands of lakes and islands. It is one of the few countries whose surface is still growing, due to rising landmasses that were once weighed down by huge ice sheets during the last ice age. Forests and ferns cover 75 percent of the land area.

Weather is the day-to-day condition of the atmosphere, whereas climate refers to the long-term average of weather. Finland is roughly divided into two climatic regions. A subarctic climate prevails in the northern half of the country, where winters are very long and cold. Temperatures can plummet to a teeth-chattering −20°F (−28°C) or colder. Summers are brief and cool, with average temperatures over 50°F (10°C) for less than four months. The southern half of the country experiences a humid, continental short summer climate; a similar climate occurs in a band extending from northern Minnesota eastward across the Great Lakes region to New England. Winters are cold, but not as fiercely so as in the north; summers are somewhat warmer, although temperatures rarely exceed 80°F (27°C). Moisture is adequate throughout the year, and drought is all but unknown.

Weather extremes in Finland are not as great—either hot or cold—as those experienced at comparable latitudes in North America or Asia. To understand why, we must once again look at a map. Have you heard of the Gulf Stream or North Atlantic current? These "rivers" flowing within the northern Atlantic Ocean transfer warm water from the equatorial latitudes northward to Europe's western shores. Additionally, seas nearly surround the country, and freshwater bodies cover much of Finland's surface. The presence of abundant water tends to moderate temperatures, making winters warmer and summers cooler than at comparable latitudes deep within continental landmasses.

You also may have heard of the Land of the Midnight Sun. Poleward of the Arctic Circle, the sun will not rise for a period of time during winter or set during summer. The precise length of time either occurs is a function of latitude. At 66½ degrees north, the sun will remain above the horizon and below the horizon for one day a year. At the North Pole (90 degrees north latitude), the duration of each condition is six months. In northern Finland, the sun remains above the horizon for about

70 days. During the long, dreary winter, however, it will stay below the horizon for a comparable length of time (although during midday, twilight conditions prevail). Even in Helsinki and elsewhere along the southern coast, summer days are about 20 hours long. During the winter, however, nights are of the same duration. For many people, the long summer days and long winter nights are much more difficult to adjust to than the severe cold.

LAND FEATURES

The Fenno-Scandian Shield, ancient worn-down rock more than 4 billion years old, forms much of Finland's land. This surface, in turn, shows the effects of ancient glacial action. As the ice sheets expanded, they acted like a bulldozer; all land lying in their path was scoured, pitted, and grooved. Ultimately, the transported rock debris was deposited to create a number of unique glacial features such as eskers (long ridges of gravel), moraines, and kames (small ridges of sand or gravel). Ice sheets tend to wear land down. As a result, most of Finland's land surface is relatively flat, low-lying, and poorly drained plains with occasional low hills. Only in the far northwestern corner of the country, near the borders with Norway and Sweden, do elevations rise. Even here, glaciers severely eroded the land and rounded off relief (difference in elevation). The country's highest peak, Haltiatunturi (Mount Haltia), rises to only 4,357 feet (1,328 meters). By comparison, this is considerably lower than the higher peaks in either the Black Hills of South Dakota or the Appalachian Mountains.

It may come as a surprise to know that Finland has nearly 180,000 islands, which is more than any other country in the world. It is estimated that 30,000 to 50,000 islands are clustered off the country's southwestern coast in the area where the gulfs of Bothnia and Finland join. Most of the islands are small and uninhabited. Even most islands owe their origin to ice-age glaciers. Many are little more than mounds of glacial debris that rise above the water; others are remnants of land left standing above surrounding lakes. Still others are the result of a process known as isostatic, or post-glacial, rebound. The tremendous weight of the ice mass forced Earth's crust downward. When the glaciers receded and the weight was removed, the land began to rise. This process has been ongoing since the end of the ice age. As a result, land once beneath the sea has emerged from the sea floor to become islands. In fact, because of this ongoing process of rebound, Finland is growing in area an estimated 2.7 square miles (7 square kilometers) each year!

The soil in Finland, generally speaking, is thin and poorly suited for agriculture. Glaciers scoured the surface, removing all preexisting soil. During the 10,000 years since they retreated, cold temperatures, abundant moisture, and an absence of sod-building grasses have combined to hinder soil development. Only about 0.02 percent of the country is farmed.

Natural Vegetation

Most of Finland, or about three-fourths of the country's land surface, is covered by dense forest. Only in the far north and far south do different vegetation patterns appear. Much of Scandinavia lies within Eurasia's vast taiga, which is the world's largest unbroken expanse of woodland. The taiga, also called the boreal forest, is largely composed of pine, spruce, larch, and fir. Larch loses its needles during the dormant season, but the other species are needle-leaf evergreen conifers. Most trees within the taiga have trunks too small to be used for lumber, but they are a valuable source of wood for pulp and paper manufacture.

Mixed forests blending to broadleaf deciduous woodlands dominated by maple, elm, alder, and aspen occur in the far south. These woodlands, however, have been cut over in many places. Here, land has been cleared for centuries to accommodate settlement and agriculture. The hardwoods also are a

Finland is Europe's most heavily forested country. In autumn, Finland's forest landscape turns into a stunning array of red and gold, known as *ruska*.

valuable natural resource for the logging and lumber industries. In the far north, tundra vegetation dominates. It features a scant cover of mosses, lichens, sedges, flowering plants, and an occasional hardy Arctic birch or stunted willow. During the short growing season, some 1,000 species of small flowering plants burst into life, creating a carpet of brilliant color. In a very short period of time, however, most such plants have completed their life cycle and have gone from seed to seed.

Animal Life

Finland has an abundance of wildlife, including 60 native mammal species. Carnivores include brown bears (the national animal), wolves, lynx, and red and Arctic foxes. The most common grazing animals are elk and reindeer. The latter is perhaps Finland's best-known animal. Technically, the reindeer is a domesticated animal that closely resembles the wild caribou. Finland's Sami (Lapps) have often been called "the Reindeer People" because of their close association with the animal. Reindeer are amazingly well adapted to cold weather. They are protected by a very dense wooly inner coat of fur and long outer coat of hollow, air-filled hairs that serve as insulators. Relative to body size, their hooves are among the largest of any animal. In winter, their hooves function much like snowshoes, allowing the animals to cross snow and ice surfaces easily. The hard edges of the hooves make it easier for the reindeer to dig beneath snow and ice for lichens and mosses. Domesticated reindeer are used in much the same way as animals in Canada and the United States. The animals provide milk, meat, and hide; they are also used to ride, carry packs, and pull sleds—including Santa's sleigh!

Birds, many of which are migratory, abound. Finland claims nearly 250 species of birds: Many are seabirds that nest on the country's many islands in the Baltic, and others are waterfowl that take advantage of the freshwater lakes and marshes. There are many woodland birds, as well, including jays, owls, hawks, and eagles. Bird watching is a popular pastime, and the country boasts many bird sanctuaries and observation posts. Finland also is home to more than 70 species of freshwater and saltwater fish. As you would expect, fishing is a very popular activity. Freshwater species such as pike, salmon, whitefish, and perch are among the most popular among anglers. Finally, Finland only has one poisonous snake, the European adder.

WATER FEATURES

From the air, Finland's surface has been described as looking like a green and blue jigsaw puzzle. Readers from Minnesota, the self-proclaimed Land of 10,000 Lakes, are in for a shock. Finland, which is only slightly larger than the state of Minnesota, has a whopping 187,888 lakes larger than 600 square yards (500 square meters). This is an area about half the size of a typical basketball court. About 12 percent of the country's surface is covered by water bodies. Added to this are huge areas of swamp and bogs (marshes) of peat. With so much standing water, mosquitoes and other insects can make life miserable for humans and animals alike during the summer months.

About 90 percent of all the world's natural lakes were formed by glaciers. Huge ice masses scoured basins, which became filled with water as they receded. The direction of glacial movement is often indicated by the orientation of water bodies (as in New York State's Finger Lakes). Many of Finland's lakes are oriented in a general northwest-southeast direction. As mentioned in the chapter introduction, most Finnish lakes are enclosed by the giant terminal moraine. This elevated feature was formed by the deposit of debris that marks the farthest extent of the last glaciation.

Despite, or perhaps because of, all of the water, Finland's thousands of rivers and smaller streams are short and present a pattern of deranged drainage, which means there is no coherent pattern to the rivers and lakes. This, too, is the result of glacial action. Mature streams with well-developed drainage basins that existed during an earlier interglacial (between periods of glaciation) were obliterated by the ice. When the glaciers receded about 10,000 years ago, new drainage patterns began to form. There was so much surface water that streams were unable to develop large drainage basins and long river courses. Additionally, the terminal moraine upon which the inner ring road was built serves as a natural dam through which very few streams flow. Streams have formed on the outer side of the moraine, but they drain small areas as they flow toward and into the sea.

The gulfs of Bothnia and Finland are extensions of the Baltic Sea, which is a unique water body. Its salinity (salt content) is the lowest of any sea that is directly connected to the global ocean. Although ocean water averages about 3.5 percent salinity, portions of the Baltic Sea are only about 0.6 percent salinity, and the sea itself averages about 1 percent salinity. Several factors account for this anomaly. First, the Baltic is semi-enclosed, having only a narrow link to the Atlantic Ocean. Second, many rivers keep a steady flow of fresh water into the Baltic Sea's basin. Finally, because of the region's cool climate, evaporation from its surface is minimal. As a result, salt accumulates very slowly. During the winter, portions of the Baltic Sea freeze over; nonetheless, commercial shipping continues year-round with lanes kept open by ice breakers when and where needed.

ENVIRONMENTAL HAZARDS AND ISSUES

Finland has very few environmental hazards, none of which can be classed as being severe in nature. At these latitudes, tornadoes and hurricanes do not occur. There are no volcanoes, and earthquakes are both few and mild. Forest fires occur occasionally, as do high winds and local flooding. Generally speaking, if you don't mind summer mosquitoes and stay clear of the country's rare venomous adder, Finland is one of the world's safest places.

Environmental issues are a relatively recent concern in Finland. This is understandable when one realizes that forests and water dominate a landscape with so few people. Since the 1970s, however, citizens have become increasingly aware of and concerned about environmental matters. Although much of it did not originate in Finland, air pollution is a problem; this, in turn, contributes to acid rain, which affects both water, with its aquatic life, and forests. Water pollution from industrial wastes and agricultural chemicals also exists. In more densely populated areas of the country, habitat destruction threatens wildlife. Since many of their environmental problems come from other countries, Finland is a party to more than 100 international environmental agreements.

3

Finland Through Time

Positioned at a precarious location on the Arctic Circle, Finland was for a long time on the edge of human activity. Why? The culture of early people simply lacked the technology to live well in this cold, somewhat hostile, and certainly unforgiving land and its environment. It was a huge challenge to meet basic needs. This eventually changed, but evidence suggests that human activity and settlement took place much later in Finland than in most other areas of the Old World. There were simply easier places to get to and live in.

Finnish culture and present society did not just happen. It evolved gradually through a path of many centuries, if not millennia. This journey brought many and varied influences to the Finns and has helped to shape the country and vibrant culture we see today. Geographers study the history of a region to help them understand the land, people, and country. Finland's path is unique to itself.

Changes introduced by both outsiders and natives within the country have contributed to the hearty culture that resides on the Arctic Circle.

This chapter focuses upon those developments that have helped to mold the character Finland exhibits today. The country's journey from the earliest peoples to the key developments of the twentieth and twenty-first centuries is fascinating, and we will learn about the men and women who have helped to develop the country. Our study will explore many important events, conflicts, and issues, including how the Finns forged a unique Finnish culture, as well as their image of this culture and the world about them. As you travel these pages, be prepared to visit a civilization that has overcome many challenges to remain independent, free, and proud of its history and culture.

EARLY PEOPLE OF FINLAND

Among the world's countries, only Iceland is wholly located as far north as Finland. This northern environment is harsh, cold, and unforgiving for much of the year. It was tougher thousands of years ago when the area was buried beneath glacial ice. For many years, scientists believed that the first people of Finland arrived about 10,000 years ago, which coincides with the retreat of glaciers from what is now Finland. In a startling discovery in 1996, geologists found evidence of earlier people in a cave called Susiluola (Wolf Cave) near Kristinestad on Finland's west coast. Archaeologists were called in and soon documented people living in the region more than 100,000 years ago. This was during the third interglacial, or warmer period, before the last ice age gripped much of northern Europe. This stunning find has caused Finland to reexamine its early roots, and research at Susiluola continues today.

Today's Finns most likely descended from people who arrived after the last ice age when the area became habitable. As the glaciers retreated northward, they left a legacy of thousands of lakes. In this post-glacial time period, tough humans were able to move into the area, adapt, and survive. These early humans were the ones described earlier who lived about 10,000 years ago. Evidence of these people has come from a weighted fishing net that was found in 1914 in a swamp at Antrea, Karelia, a region that the Finns once controlled, but lost to the Soviet Union in 1940. Other discoveries of early humans come also from the same time period in the community of Lahti, which is located northeast of Helsinki.

These early people were hunters and gatherers who used stone tools; they are believed to have come from present-day Estonia, which is located to the south, across the Gulf of Finland, and from central Russia to the southeast. Later people made weapons fashioned out of stone and bone. For survival, they fished and hunted animals common to the area, such as elk, beaver, and seal. Settlements were always near the vital resource: water.

Around 5,000 B.C., Finland's climate began to warm, and precipitation increased. This allowed people to use their environment in new ways, as trees and other new plants were introduced naturally, creating new food, fuel, and housing sources. Archaeologists have discovered pottery from this era, introduced from Russia. Neolithic Finns decorated their pottery in distinctive and ornamental styles including the common Combed Ware. In this style, they dragged combs across soft clay to create parallel lines left as a design when the pottery hardens. More people moved into Finland from central Russia around 4,000 B.C., and people at this time spoke a type of Finno-Ugric language. The Ugric roots traced back to the ancestors of the Magyars of Hungary. Most of these early Finnish tribal settlements were established along the coast of the Gulf of Finland. Because the country continues to rise (see Chapter 2 for an explanation), many of these early settlement sites are now located several miles inland.

A little before 3,000 B.C., people from the Baltic region started to move into Finland. They also brought their language, and these influences contributed to changes in the existing language that eventually evolved into the Baltic-Finnish language family. Combed Ware had also evolved further by this era, but people continued to hunt, fish, and gather to feed themselves. By this time, only the dog had been domesticated. This all began to change with the introduction of agriculture to the region around 2,300 B.C. The Suomalaiset tribe was living in southwest Finland; Suomi, the Finns' name for their country, came from this tribe. North of the Suomi were the Sami or Lapps who lived in Finland's frigid north. This group sought to preserve their autonomy and never wanted to assimilate with the Finns in the south. The Sami language was also Finno-Ugric, but little is known about their early prehistory culture, as they had little contact with people located farther south.

By 1,500 B.C., the Bronze Age had arrived in Finland from Russia, and the Iron Age arrived a thousand years later, as iron blades from this era have been found. During the intervening time, trade had developed around the Baltic Sea as the exchanges of goods and ideas picked up speed. Religion entered the Finnish scene, and new procedures were used to bury the dead under cairns of stone. A cairn is a human-constructed pile of stones; in Finland, they were used to mark a burial location. Finland seems to have borrowed the idea of burial cairns from Sweden, their neighbor to the west and north.

Since Finland's recorded history began during the twelfth century, knowledge of the many elements of the past that took place after the birth of Christ are sketchy. However, in A.D. 98, a Roman historian named Tacitus wrote about a Fenni tribe in the far north of Europe. His descriptions were rather unflattering, as he called them wild savages who were poor and didn't have horses, weapons, or even houses. No one is certain whether he was referring to the Sami, those who were there before them, or to other Finns in the south; however, most believe Tacitus was describing the Lapps in the north. This is considered to be the first written reference about the Finns.

During the Bronze Age (1300 B.C.–500 B.C.), newcomers from Scandinavia reached the southwest coast of Finland, bringing with them a new religion and burial customs. These new inhabitants buried their dead people under cairns (stone monuments), which were built on high rocks close to the sea.

In the first millennium, tribes in southern Finland traded with the Vikings from Sweden and Estonia. These Finnish tribes were mainly the Tavastians in the west and central regions, and the Karelians in the east. Karelians are the forerunners of the Finns, and the Tavastians are a group often forgotten in an examination of Finland's past. The Tavastians were culturally very similar to the Karelians, but the two were considered to be different tribes and frequently were at war with each other. Partial evidence of this comes from the hill-forts that are more commonly found in Tavastian-occupied areas. One distinguishing characteristic seems to be that the Tavastians were more warlike than the Karelians. Another difference is that the Tavastians were considered to be pagan, while the Karelians were already being influenced by Christianity. A strong outside influence would soon affect their eastward quest for expansion: The Swedes were about to enter Finland in a major way.

SWEDISH RULE AND INFLUENCE

With their close proximity, Finland and farther east were natural directions for the expansionist-minded Swedes to venture. Recorded history allows us to understand this time period better than earlier times when history had not been written. The Swedes were searching for trade routes to Russia, the Black Sea, and ultimately to the Arab world, and Finland was a natural stopping point. Soon, the Swedes became the dominant force in the region. They began to influence, although some would say force their culture upon, the tribal Finns. At this time, it is estimated that there were only 50,000 Finns, so Swedish domination was not difficult to achieve.

During this era, the Catholic Church was in disarray and splitting into factions either loyal to the pope of Rome or to the patriarch of Constantinople. This split is referred to as the Great Schism, a conflict that served as one of many divisions between the east and west. By 1054, as the conflict heated, the two factions had excommunicated each other. Both then sent out armies of missionaries to win or force converts. Thus, Finland was caught in the middle. Finns were being pressed by the Swedish Catholic faith coming from the west, but from the east, the Greek Catholic (to become the Greek Orthodox) Church was also interested in spreading its beliefs to Finland.

These early Finns found themselves caught politically and geographically between two powerful forces. Both the Swedes and Russians were busily imposing their imprint on the land and people. The Finns were also on the front lines of battle between the soon-to-be Greek Orthodox and Roman Catholic faiths. This meant that the country had truly become a religious battlefield between the Swedish Catholic faith and the Byzantine Catholic Church, which was a precursor to the Orthodox faith. Thus, nearly 1,000 years ago, tiny fragile Finland was on the front lines in the struggles between the east and west. As a result, many of the Finns in the east and in Karelia became Orthodox, while Finns in the west became Swedish Catholics.

The process of Swedish domination may have started in earnest in 1155. In that year, legend tells us that Swedish king Erik IX ordered Bishop Henry, an Englishman, to accompany him on a Roman Catholic Christian crusade to Finland. Although Christianity had been introduced earlier, it had not been forced upon the Finns, as the Swedes were about to do. Beginning in southwest Finland, Henry initiated Swedish colonization and forced baptism on the local populations. In 1156, an angry peasant named Lalli killed Henry, allegedly because the bishop had misbehaved at his home. Today, it is still unknown whether this story is true. In any case, Bishop Henry is considered the patron saint of Finland, and Christianity was widely introduced into the country around this time.

This was not the end of the religious conflict in Finland, as Rome sanctioned a number of Swedish crusades into the eastern regions in the thirteenth century. The first two efforts started in 1240 and 1242, but both were turned back by the Russians. The Swedes attempted a third crusade in 1293, but this too failed to take Russian-held Karelia. The third crusade resulted in the peace treaty of Pähkinäsaari, 30 years later in 1323, which created a border between Russian-controlled Karelia and Finland that lasted for almost three centuries. This border became the dividing line between the Orthodox east and the Catholic west.

Sweden controlled most of the central and western portions of Finland by this time and ruled them as a part of Sweden. Swedish rule would last more than 650 years until 1809 when Finland became an autonomous state under Russia. In earlier times, most Finns lived near the coast, but under Swedish rule, they eventually started to move inland and began to farm. The Swedish rulers, who gave away large tracts of land and granted tax favors, hoped to encourage people to settle in the remote frontier areas of the country. As people moved farther north, conflicts developed with the Lapps, who herded reindeer and were accustomed to moving around freely with their animals. Thus, as in the American West where farmers with fences were in sharp conflict with open ranges and free movement and live-stock, problems also developed in medieval Finland between farmers and herders.

Early-Finnish farmers had a challenging situation. They had to clear lands of trees, and the soil they worked was of marginal quality at best. In addition, as a result of the northern and increasingly inland farming, the growing season was very short. This meant that most farmers needed to supplement their crops by hunting, fishing, and gathering.

Medieval Finland had developed into a society with four social classes: a small number of nobility at the top, followed by the clergy, burghers (middle class), and finally, at the bottom, peasants. Although most of the Finns were peasants who spoke the Finnish language, the educated and upper classes spoke Swedish.

More communities were established during the medieval era, with many structures still evident today. One example, started in 1475, is Olavinlinna Castle, a beautiful fortress on a small island in the city of Savonlinna, which is situated between two lakes. The castle is still used today and serves as the host site for the world-famous Savonlinna Opera Festival that is staged each summer.

THE KALMAR UNION

Queen Margaret I of Denmark encouraged a unity of Scandi-navian areas in the late fourteenth century as Germans began to encroach upon the region. Through marriage, she gained control of Norway when her husband, Olaf, died in 1387. This was the start of the Scandinavian Empire called the Kalmar Union. Queen Margaret then built alliances with Swedish nobility who were dissatisfied with King Albert of Mecklen-burg. In 1388, she was elected as the Swedish sovereign. King Albert tried to retake his throne by force, but the effort failed miserably in 1389. Queen Margaret died in 1412, but she was responsible for uniting the Kalmar Union, which effectively lasted until 1523. In that year, Gustav Vasa, a Swedish noble, led a successful revolt against the Danes; this again made Sweden, including Finland, independent. Gustav Vasa was elected king of Sweden in 1523.

FINLAND AND THE REFORMATION

Events that took place in Europe to the south of Finland con-tinued to have an impact on the country during the sixteenth century. In 1517, Martin Luther, a German religious leader and reformer, had published his *Ninety-five Theses on the Power and Efficacy of Indulgences*. In this document, he criticized the excesses and indulgences of the Catholic Church and, as a result, initiated the Protestant Reformation. This movement first tried to reform the Catholic Church, but later it sparked a total split from Rome. Sweden embraced the reform movement in 1527 when King Gustav Vasa seized most of the property of the Catholic Church and adopted the Lutheran faith. Finland had its own reformation inspiration, sparked by Mikael Agricola, a Finn who had studied with Martin Luther in Germany. Later, in 1548, he became the first person to translate the Bible's New Testament into Finnish. Today he is celebrated by Finns not only as a religious leader, but also as the father of written Finn-ish, as his works were the first to be printed in the language.

Under King Gustav I, Sweden extended its control over Fin-land. He founded the cities of Helsinki, the capital of Finland today, and Ekenas (Tammisaari in Finnish), both of which are located on the southern coast of the Gulf of Finland. Has the Swedes' influence been lasting? Surprisingly, yes, as even today 83 percent of the population in Ekenas speaks Swedish as their

King Gustav Vasa I was crowned king of Sweden in 1523 after leading a successful revolt against Christian II of Denmark, the leader of the Kalmar Union and most of Sweden. Founder of the Vasa dynasty and unifier of Sweden, he built a strong monarchy and an efficient administration.

primary language. Helsinki is today the country's largest city, with a population of about 550,000. Nearly a million people live in the capital and surrounding metropolitan area that includes the cities of Espoo, Vantaa, and Kauniainen. However, only about 6 percent of the people in the capital now speak Swedish. Intermarriage with Finns and the societal preference for the Finnish language in daily life have taken a toll on the use of the Swedish language.

THE BALTIC WARS

While Gustav I extended the reach of Sweden in Finland and other areas around the Baltic Sea, he wisely avoided costly wars. This was not the case with his successors. Other powers around the Baltic Sea, such as Poland, Denmark, and Finland's huge eastern neighbor, Russia, closely watched Sweden's quiet quest for an empire. During the last three centuries of Swedish rule in Finland, more than one-quarter of the time was spent in wars with one or more of the other Baltic powers. These struggles were violent winner-take-all skirmishes with the following being most notable:

- **Russo-Swedish War** (1570–1595): Finns called this war, which was fought between Sweden and Russia for more than a quarter of a century, the Long Wrath. Finns, caught in the middle of these two powers, were conscripted to fight on behalf of Sweden. The Long Wrath ended with most of Finland's settlements destroyed by fire. The Treaty of Tyavzino ended the sacking of Finland with the Russians gaining some lands.

- **The Thirty Years' War** (1618–1648): This battle was between Sweden, other countries, and the Habsburg Empire that was encroaching upon the possessions of others on the Baltic. Most of the fighting was done in Germany. Finns were again conscripted to fight for Sweden in the series of conflicts that ended in 1648 with the Peace of Westphalia. The end of this series of wars left Sweden as one of the major powers in Europe.

King Gustav II Adolf was also known as "Lion of the North" and the "Father of Modern Warfare." Admired for his leadership and innovative military skills during the Thirty Years' War, future commanders such as Napoleon Bonaparte of France and Carl von Clausewitz of Prussia considered him one of the greatest generals of all time. Every year Sweden celebrates Gustav Adolf Day on November 6.

- **The Great Northern War** (1700–1721): Poland,
  Denmark, and Russia worked together in an alliance to break up the Swedish Empire at a time
  when they thought the Swedes were vulnerable. The
  Finns also had suffered in 1696 with a devastating
  famine during which about one-third of the population died of starvation. Thus, with diminished
  strength the Swedes, including the Finns, lost major
  ground in this conflict. Finland suffered horribly
  from 1714–1722 when the Russians occupied their
  lands. Finns refer to this period as the Great Wrath,
  because nearly one-fifth of the population tragically
  died during the war. The war ended with the Peace
  of Uusikaupunki in which the Swedes lost lands
  on the southern and eastern coasts of the Baltic
  Sea. After the war, most of Finland was still held by
  Sweden, although some Finnish lands had been lost
  to Russia in the southeast. By the end of the Great
  Northern War, Russia had established itself as the
  strongest power on the Baltic Sea.

- **Russo-Swedish War** (1741–1743): This conflict was
  a rematch as the Swedes sought to regain lands lost
  in the Great Northern War. Unfortunately for the
  Swedes, they lost again. As a result, more Finnish
  lands in the southeast fell to Russia, although the
  Russians withdrew from most Finnish lands. Finns
  refer to this war and the second Russian occupation
  as the Lesser Wrath.

- **Russo-Swedish War** (1788–1790): Sweden again
  tried to recoup lost lands by declaring war on Russia. By this time, some Finns were tired of being
  a battlefield for the wars between the Russians to
  the east and the Swedes to the west. Finnish offi-
  cers referred to as the Anjala League led a mutiny;

the mutiny was put down, as the league wanted to avoid Russian punishment again. Finns today view the efforts of the Anjala League as the first steps toward the creation of a Finnish nation.

- **The Finnish War** (1808–1809): This war was the final saga in the series of conflicts between the Swedes and Russians. Russia overran Finland in 1809. The Treaty of Hamina granted Finland to Russia and ended the Swedes' domination of Finland. The transition introduced a new Russian master, and it also marked the establishment of the semiautonomous Grand Duchy of Finland that will be discussed later.

SWEDISH REMNANTS IN FINLAND

Sweden's long governance of Finland led not only to frequent wars but also to other cultural contributions that still exist in the country today. Six hundred and fifty years of Swedish rule left many imprints upon the culture of Finland. Some have already been discussed, such as the religious influence and the Swedish language that is spoken, even today, by many Finns.

The Finnish Lutheran Church is the country's dominant faith, claiming nearly 85 percent of the population. Thus, the Swedes effectively disseminated the Lutheran faith to Finland, where it remains very strong today. The Finnish branch is now the world's third largest Lutheran group. The religious influences also extend to holidays, such as Christmas and Easter, which are celebrated in Finland.

Both Swedish and Finnish have been adopted as Finland's official languages, and the Swedish language is still the primary tongue of nearly 6 percent of the population. One-third of these people speak only Swedish, and nearly two dozen communities still use Swedish as their primary language. About 6 percent of the country's population is composed of ethnic Swedes, who mostly reside in these towns. Swedish has also influenced the Finnish language, since Finnish has adopted many Swedish words, especially in urban areas like Helsinki. The strength of Swedish in the country is further demonstrated by the fact that 15 daily newspapers are printed in Swedish.

Even though many Finns hesitate to admit it, Sweden has also made other lasting contributions. Many of their administrative and educational structures were adapted and used by the Finns. Perhaps the greatest cultural influence of the Swedes was during the eighteenth century, when Swedish influences were prevalent among the elite. This was the era when the Finnish language and culture was for the peasants, and the educated higher classes preferred the Swedish language and culture. Despite the influences of Sweden, however, the results of the Finnish War brought a new master to Finland. How would this new master rule over the Finns? The next chapter will investigate the complex relationship that developed between Finland and Russia.

CHAPTER

4

Caught Between Powers and Independence

Pressed between two powers for centuries, Finland found itself under the authority of the Russian Bear in 1809. The era of Swedish dominance had passed, but now Russia was the new overlord. At first, Russia planned to annex Finland into its territory and make it a new province. The feisty Finns resisted this complete integration into Russia, so Finland was instead personally attached to the tsar of Russia. With this arrangement, Finland became the Grand Duchy of Finland and retained its earlier constitution and laws. The tsar replaced the king of Sweden as Finland's monarch. In addition, Russia allowed the Finns to keep their traditions. With these concessions and lost lands returned to Finland, the Finns actually became very accepting of the new rulers. Finland was autonomous. The ability to regain lost lands and maintain their government structure and traditions made it easier to accept the sovereignty of the Russian tsar Alexander I. Russia still was the real power, but the Finns were somewhat independent; of even greater importance, Finland was at peace for the first time in centuries. Unfortunately, the Grand Duchy only lasted until 1917.

It was during the long Russian era that the roots of Finnish nationalism were planted. The Finnish language became stronger as resistance to the Swedish language grew. In 1812, the Russians moved Finland's capital to Helsinki. The city expanded its influence even further when the country's only university, at Turku, was transferred to Helsinki in 1828. Soon the university became the center for Finnish nationalism. The Russians supported the Finnish language movement at first, since it helped them to remove Swedish influences. The Finnish language nationalism movement was soon to be called the Fennoman movement as it increasingly took on political aspects. Some of these new dimensions included Finnish nationalism and even the idea of independence. Soon, Russia was much less enchanted with the new efforts of the Fennoman movement and other nationalists.

In 1899, a major turning point occurred when the Russian tsar, Nicholas II, issued a new policy called the February Manifesto, which extended Russian rule in Finland and virtually made it a province. Finns were furious, as they believed that this directly broke the promise of Tsar Alexander I to allow the Finns to have their own constitution and traditions. Quickly the Finns gathered petitions against the manifesto and garnered over a half-million signatures. In response, the tsar rejected the petitions by simply ignoring them. Two years later, in 1901, Russia usurped the Finnish Army and conscripted Finns as soldiers. This united the Finns even more against Russian rule and further fomented Finnish nationalism. Finns were also fleeing the country in record numbers to emigrate to the United States and Canada. Nearly one-third million Finns left the country between 1864 and 1914.

Russia began to have its own internal problems in the early twentieth century, as labor revolts there also affected Finland.

During the Finnish civil war, acts of terror were committed by both sides. Although the Whites and the Reds had agreed on certain rules of engagement, violations occurred from the start. In Red-dominated areas businessmen, landowners, and other members of the middle class were murdered for political reasons. The White Guards executed Red party leaders, prisoners of war, and Russian soldiers who fought with the Red Guards.

Seizing the moment, the Finns pressured for more independence in governance. This effort advanced in 1906 when the tsar encouraged Finland to form a unicameral (one-house) parliament. This allowed for the creation of the first Eduskunta (parliament). The same year, the country implemented universal suffrage, which gave all adults, including women, the right to vote. This historic act made Finland Europe's first country to extend voting rights to women. By 1908, however, Russia was again trying to tighten its grip on Finland, and the Finnish constitution had again been greatly crippled by 1914.

When the Russian Revolution broke out in March 1917, its effects quickly spread to Finland. On December 6 of the same year, Finland declared its independence from Russia. A violent Finnish civil war followed: One group, the Reds, was linked to Russia's Bolsheviks (Communists), and another faction, the Whites, had the support of Imperial Germany. In a war that lasted only a few months, 30,000 Finns died. Another 300,000 fled, most emigrating to the United States. The Whites won the war, which ended in 1918, but animosity remained between the factions that had split during the fighting. After the war, a German nobleman was nominated to be king of Finland, but he refused to accept the role.

FINLAND BETWEEN WARS

In 1919, the Finnish Eduskunta adopted a new constitution that established a republican form of government. This constitution was used until 2000, when it was replaced by a new document. In 1920, Finland joined the League of Nations as the fledgling Finns began to participate in world affairs as an independent country. Still looming to the east was the hulking, now communist, former Russia with a new name: the Soviet Union. Fear of a Soviet attack was very high. Finns realized that maintaining their independence would require vigilance, as this huge and powerful neighbor maintained a strong interest in Finland; as a result, Finns strongly distrusted the Soviets.

Several treaties had been signed with the Russians, including a ten-year nonaggression pact in 1932, but the Finns still did not trust the Soviets, and they continued to explore other options that would help to keep them independent. To counter the Soviet threat, Finland sought alliances that would balance the Soviets and prevent them from invading again. Since the Soviet Union feared a German attack, the Finns played on this fear by appearing to have a close relationship with Germany.

After independence, the civil strife in Finland also continued, as the overflow of the Russian Revolution continued with the Reds and Whites skirmishing. Conflicts between Finns and Swedes also took place between the two world wars. In spite of the continuing unrest, a Finn long-distance runner, Paavo Nurmi, won nine gold and three silver medals over three Olympic games. Finns from all factions celebrated his incredible achievements; he later earned the privilege of lighting the Olympic flame in Helsinki when the summer games were hosted there in 1952. Nurmi remains a national hero in Finland today.

Finally, the Finnish civil war ended, and both political and social compromises were reached. Scars remained, but many things helped to heal the country: the 1919 constitution, the formation of new political parties, and a law that made Swedish and Finnish both official national languages.

Soon after 1922, industries were developing as the economy started to grow. Lumber led the way, with mining and foreign trade aiding the development. The country's conservative fiscal policies were a key element in helping Finland advance economically, and the country avoided debt on both the domestic and international fronts. In addition, the country was progressive in protecting its workers and citizens. Insurance helped the aged, children, and the handicapped as the country started to provide for the social welfare of its citizens.

THE RUSSIANS ARE COMING! THE RUSSIANS ARE COMING!

Without warning or a declaration of war, the Soviets attacked Finland on November 30, 1939. The Germans, who had signed the Nazi-Soviet Non-Aggression Pact earlier in 1939, aided

Fast-moving ski troops in white camouflage suits fought under harsh conditions during the Winter War. Soviet leader Joseph Stalin had expected to quickly defeat Finland, but Finnish troops held off the Soviets for 100 days. The Finns were eventually defeated and signed over 10 percent of its territory to the Soviet Union.

this sneak attack. This agreement contained a secret provision whereby Germany and the Soviet Union granted each other "spheres of influence." For Finland, this meant that Germany had sold them out; the Soviets could now proceed against the Finns, without German resistance. This conflict was called the Winter War of 1939–1940 and was the first between Finland and the Soviet Union during World War II.

The fierce Finns fought valiantly during the Winter War, under incredibly horrible conditions. Temperatures plunged to −40°F (−40°C). Thousands died fighting during the harsh winter, which was one of the worst of the twentieth century. After 100 days, the brave Finns lost to the Soviets. With this defeat, they were forced to give up a part of Karelia that was ceded to the Soviet Union.

After this painful defeat, the Finns approached Hitler's Germany for assistance. A treaty called the German-Finnish Agreement was signed in 1940. With this pact, German troops were allowed to move through Finland by train and were on Finnish soil when the second Finnish-Soviet War took place. The Soviets had looked somewhat inept in their costly victory over Finland in the Winter War. As a result, Germany's Adolf Hitler believed that he could successfully invade the Soviet Union. The Germans attacked the Soviet Union on June 22, 1941, and, in response, the Soviets attacked the Finns again. Finland responded by declaring war on the Soviet Union on June 26, 1941. This second conflict between Finland and the Soviet Union, called the Continuation War, lasted from 1941–1944, and the Finns were defeated again. Borders were mostly the same as the 1940 agreement, but German troops were ordered out of Finland. The Communist Party, which had been outlawed in 1930, was allowed to operate again in the country. Although the Soviets again won the war, they still did not occupy Finland.

Unfortunately, fighting related to World War II was not yet over for Finland. Germany was afraid that Finland might reach an agreement with the Soviets. In particular, they wanted to protect the Finnish mines that they controlled in the country's remote north. When the Finns signed their agreement with the Soviet Union in 1944, they agreed to have German troops removed from Finland. Thus, fighting once again broke out, this time in northern Finland. The war that followed was called the Lapland War, which Finland won in 1945. Yes, the Finns were finally victorious!

The era of wars in Finland came at a great cost to the country. It is believed that 86,000 Finns died, with tens of thousands of others injured and maimed. Another half million were refugees who had fled from the fighting and advancing armies. In addition to lost lands, Finland had to pay the equivalent of $300 million in reparations to the Soviet Union (mostly paid with hardware, like ships and machinery). Unfortunately, the country once again found itself twisting uncomfortably under a high degree of Soviet influence over the country's politics and society. Thus, at the end of World War II, the Russian Bear still loomed as a dangerous presence over Finland.

AFTER WORLD WAR II

After World War II, Finland was again pinched between East and West. This time it wasn't between Sweden and Russia; rather, it was between the Soviet Union and its satellite countries to the east and the United States with its allies in the west. Finland was now on the front lines of the Cold War. Although fiercely independent, the Finns knew that they needed to accommodate the Soviets while, at the same time, maintaining their political independence. This presented a delicate balancing act that would require much of this fragile Scandinavian country. What was the new plan? Friendship!

The Finns had learned the hard way that hostility toward the Soviet Union did not work well. Thus, friendship was the new path as they signed the Treaty of Friendship, Cooperation, and Mutual Assistance with the Soviet Union in 1948. Finland was now officially neutral, as the treaty was extended in 1955, 1970, and 1983. With the crumbling of the Soviet Union in the early 1990s, the treaty was declared null and void. A new treaty was signed, however, to promote good relations and to lessen the threat of military intervention.

Finland's neutrality and independence provided many new opportunities after World War II. The country hosted the Summer Olympics in 1952 and joined the United Nations in 1955. Finland joined the European Free Trade Association in 1986, the Council of Europe in 1989, and the European Union in 1995. These developments and others have contributed to Finland's rapid economic development. Today, the country has a vibrant market economy and is very technologically advanced.

In 2006, Finland celebrated the one-hundredth anniversary of its unicameral parliament—100 years of voting and democracy despite the country's location in between the East and West during the Cold War. Even the Soviet Union couldn't tame the Finns' thirst for democracy, freedom, and independence. Over their history, the fiercely independent Finns have prevailed against an extremely harsh environment and hostile neighbors. Is there any question that they will continue to defy all odds in the future?

5

People and Culture

Finland's people are called Finns, or the Finnish people. Their traits are varied, but certain trends and patterns are evident. Some are rather confusing, as they seem to be disconnected. For example, Finns have one of the world's highest standards of living and a strong government social support system, yet alcoholism and suicide are rampant. Finnish men have the highest suicide rate in Western Europe, and alcohol consumption is a major contributing factor. This connection is also true of youth aged 13–22. Studies have found that 42 percent of the suicides are linked to alcohol, and the country is one of the world's leading nations in binge drinking by youth. In 2005, it was found that alcohol was the leading cause of death for Finns between the ages of 15 and 64. Finns also lead the world in coffee consumption.

Even with the addictive behaviors noted here, Finns rate themselves as being very happy. According to world rankings in 2006, Finns were the sixth happiest people in the world (Canadians placed fourth, and Americans placed nineteenth) in terms of overall satisfaction. What a confusing situation! Why does a seemingly happy and prosperous country have such high rates of addictive behaviors and suicide? It is a difficult question to answer. This chapter further investigates the intriguing people and culture of Finland in an attempt to learn more about possible answers.

POPULATION

By international standards, Finland has a small population, which was estimated in mid-2007 to be 5,238,460, about the same as Arizona or Maryland, or a little more than the Canadian city of Toronto. With a land area of 130,558.5 square miles (338,145 square kilometers), the country is a little smaller than the U.S. state of Montana, or Labrador and Newfoundland in Canada.

As a result of the country's northern location, much of the land has been difficult to settle because of the cold winters. This means that most people and urban centers are located in the southern part of the country, where the climate is milder. The population density for the country as a whole is only 40 people per square mile (15 per square kilometer) but the rate varies greatly from the north to the south. For example, the province of Uusimaa, which includes Helsinki, has a population density of 531 people per square mile (205 per square kilometer). In stark contrast, Lapland has a population density of only 6 people per square mile (2 per square kilometer.). This disparity in population creates a number of challenges for the people and their government, as the needs of southern urban and northern more isolated populations can vary widely.

Population Characteristics

Statistical information on Finland reflects a prosperous and well-educated population with characteristics similar to those of other well-developed countries. For example, the average lifespan is quite high. Men have a life expectancy at birth of 75 years and women of 82 years. A combined life expectancy of 78.7 years places Finland in the top 20 percent of the world's countries. Finland has the world's fifth lowest infant mortality rate, with only 3.52 per 1000 live births. The fertility rate, which is the average number of children born to a woman, is very low at 1.73. This is well below the replacement rate of 2.1 children per woman. Nonetheless, because of immigration, the country's population continues to grow at 0.13 percent per year. The Population Reference Bureau (PRB) projects that Finland will have 5.3 million people in the year 2050. This is virtually the same number as today.

An upcoming challenge for the Finns is that the average age of its population is increasing. While the median (middle) age of the world's population is 27.6 years, the median for Finns is 41.6 years. This aging population makes it more difficult to find workers to replace older employees who retire. This condition will have many other economic and social implications for the country. The government realizes the problem and the need to either provide incentives for larger families, take steps to increase immigration, or support both options.

Other data show that Finns are very well educated and financially successful. The literacy rate is a perfect 100 percent for people over 15 years of age. Additionally, the per-capita Gross Domestic Product (GDP) was $37,460 according to the World Bank in 2006. This figure was the eleventh highest in the world. HIV/AIDS rates are very low, at under 0.1 percent. Other factors indicating a high quality of life are offered by the PRB, which shows that 100 percent of Finns have adequate sanitation, and all Finnish women have medical professionals present at childbirth.

In addition, Finns have universal access to health care. This means that all people have medical care provided to them by the government. Many claim that the Finns' health-care system is the most comprehensive in the world today. The system is paid for by taxes and is implemented locally. Finns consistently report that they are very happy with their health-care system; in Europe, only the Danes report higher satisfaction with their system. In 2006, Finland ranked eleventh among countries in the annual United Nations Human Development Index (HDI) Report.

Ethnicity

Finland is a very homogeneous country in terms of ethnic diversity, where 93.4 percent of the population is Finnish. Few countries in the world have less diverse populations. Other ethnic groups do exist in Finland, but in small numbers. The second largest ethnic group is Swedes, with 5.7 percent of the population. Their historical ties to Finland have left a Swedish population that maintains its language and many other cultural practices. Other smaller ethnic groups in Finland include Russians (0.4 percent); Estonians (0.2 percent); Roma, or Gypsies (0.2 percent); and the Sami, or Lapps (0.1 percent).

The Sami are Finland's (and Scandinavia's) indigenous (native) people. In the past they were referred to as Lapps, people who lived in Lapland, a region located in the northern parts of Finland, Sweden, and Norway. Today, however, many Sami consider the term *Lapp* to be derogatory and prefer to be called Sami. Two cities in Finland with significant Sami populations are Rovaniemi and Inari. Today only about 4,000 Sami live in Finland, but some 30,000 are scattered across Lapland. With their own cultural heritage, the Sami today still bolster their economy by making *duodji* (traditional handicrafts). They also hunt, herd reindeer, and fish, all of which continue to involve some traditional practices. Reindeer have played a major role in traditional Sami culture. Even today, nearly 10 percent of them rely primarily on reindeer as their primary source of income.

There are ten different Sami languages spread across Lapland, and three of these are spoken in Finland. Most of

Reindeer have been herded for centuries by the Samis, the first inhabitants of Finland. Raised for their meat, hide, antlers, and formerly for milk and transportation, they generally roam free on pasture grounds. Today, sauteed reindeer is the best-known dish in Lapland.

the Sami people also speak their national language, which is specific to the life and culture of the Sami. For example, there are over 400 Sami words for reindeer. Yet, at the same time, the Sami of today have also adopted many cultural practices from the Finns, Russians, Swedes, and Norwegians.

Finland's Swedish- and Russian-speaking populations have evolved out of the country's long-term involvement with these neighboring countries. As is described elsewhere, frequent wars and conflicts often left either the Swedes or Russians in control of Finland. As a result of these conflicts, many Russians and Swedes decided to stay and live in Finland. Some Russians also fled that country after the Russian Revolution and sought refuge in Finland. Both native languages are actively used by many of the Swedes and Russians in Finland, but most also speak Finnish today.

The first Roma people, or Gypsies, arrived in Finland during the sixteenth century. More recent immigration has also taken place since the 1960s. Today there are about 10,000 Roma in the country. Roma people in Finland and elsewhere across Europe often hold cultural values that are in conflict with those of the dominant culture, which often results in prejudice and discrimination against the Roma. Finland's Roma population has a high rate of unemployment, and their living conditions are poor. The Roma mostly live in major cities in southern Finland. Both the Finnish government and European Union have undertaken major efforts to improve economic opportunities for Roma people, along with protecting their political and civil rights.

Tartars, who started to arrive during the late nineteenth century, are another small ethnic group in Finland. They are the oldest Muslim group in Finland, and there are only about 1,000 of them in the country today. These are Turkish people, and they are well integrated into Finnish society. Many still practice their Turkic language, and most live in or near the city of Helsinki.

FINNISH CULTURE

The dominant way of life in Finland is, of course, the Finnish culture, as this group comprises the vast majority of the population, with over five million people. The culture is expressed in a variety of ways, many of which will be explored in this chapter. Many cultural elements also have been borrowed from their Swedish neighbors to the west and their Russian neighbors

to the east. Other elements have come from the Finns themselves. For example, in conversation, the people tend to be no-
nonsense folks who have little time for small talk. Words are
usually used carefully, and discussions focus upon important
matters—except in the sauna. We will now take a closer look at
the Finns and some of the characteristics of their culture. First
is the Finnish sauna.

The sauna represents a key element in Finnish culture and
one that is a profound expression of their triumph over their
cold climate. These unique "sweat bathhouses" are almost
sacred places to the Finns; in fact, there are about two million
of them in the country, nearly one for every two people! This
national pastime is viewed as a cleansing of both the mind and
body, as well as a healing and spiritual retreat.

The traditional sauna is a wooden building separate from
the home. Today, however, they are included in many modern
buildings, including the Finnish Parliament. The sauna is a
place for relaxation; it is usually forbidden to talk of politics,
religion, and other weighty matters. Bathers do not usually
wear clothes, but it is not a sexual place, as that would violate
the sanctity of the sauna. Older men and women generally
bathe separately in the sauna, unless they are with their imme-
diate family. Younger Finns may often have men and women in
the sauna together as the tradition changes. It is hot! Often the
water is heated to a nearly boiling temperature. After a time in
the sauna, bathers will often take a quick dive into a freezing
lake or swimming pool. Then they go back to the sauna and
repeat the cycle two to three times in a ritual that can take two
hours or more.

Finns also have a very strong national identity, and they are
proud of their country and heritage. After centuries of being
occupied and used as a battlefield between the Russians and
Swedes, they are fiercely independent but pragmatic. Finns
take exceptional pride in their athletes, authors, artists, achievements, and economy.

During the past century, Finland and Sweden have been fierce rivals in men's ice hockey. At the 2006 Winter Olympics, Finland's Leijonat (the Lions) came close to winning the final, but was eventually defeated 3-2 by Sweden. They brought home the silver medal.

Sports are very popular with Finns; they enjoy everything from Formula One race-car driving to a sport called *pesapallo.* Pesapallo is also often referred to as Finnish baseball, with rules that are very similar, and the game is the country's national sport. Other favored sports include ice hockey, track and field, skiing, fishing, hunting, Nordic walking, soccer, and jogging. Finns are active both as fans and as participants. The government has encouraged greater involvement in sports, as the problem of obesity has increased greatly in the country over the past decade. The Finnish sense of humor also comes out at the Finnwacky events that will be described in Chapter 7. Culture is far broader than the items discussed thus far, so it is time to investigate other areas of Finnish culture in greater depth, beginning with the array of arts that have flourished.

Arts

A culture's arts provide expressions that appeal to a variety of the senses. For example, music appeals to the ears, but it can be combined with dance so that the visual is also included. Paintings and architecture appeal to the eyes, while plays and films are both seen and heard. The arts come in many forms, and Finland has its own rich cultural heritage.

Literature is one form of the arts, and Finnish literature has roots going back to Mikael Agricola, who is considered to be the father of the written Finnish language. He translated parts of the Bible in connection with the Protestant Reformation in the sixteenth century. Caught between Sweden and Russia and the ongoing political struggles, literature didn't really begin to flourish in Finland until the nineteenth century. Elias Lönnrot began to collect the poetry of Finnish writers and compiled them into a book of folklore called the *Kalevala.* This work has become a national epic that has influenced music and the fine arts and has been translated into nearly 50 languages. Other writers like Mika Waltari and Aleksis Kivi became popular in the twentieth century, along with F.E. Sillanpää, who won a Nobel Prize for literature in 1939. His powerful descriptions of rural landscapes almost overpowered the characters in his writings. Not surprisingly, a common setting for many characters in Finnish literature is in the sauna.

Inspired by the writings in the *Kalevala*, Jean Sibelius, a Finnish music composer wrote a vocal symphony called the *Kullervo* in the last decade of the nineteenth century. In this symphony, Sibelius captured the national spirit of the *Kalevala,* and he was also inspired by the landscape of the country that he loved so much. His music supported the rise of Finnish nationalism in the early twentieth century that resulted in Finland's independence in 1917. Writing classical music is still a popular endeavor in Finland today, as important composers like Magnus Lindberg and Einojuhani Rautavaara are still writing.

In contrast, Finns also enjoy heavy metal rock music, which is performed enthusiastically by local bands. Many of these groups also are popular across Europe and some, like Nightwish and HIM, even have strong followings in Canada and the United States. HIM was the first Finnish group to have a gold album (sales of over 500,000) in the United States, and it has toured with international groups like Metallica. Other popular bands include Amorphis, Bomfunk MC'S, The Crash, The Rasmus, Finntroll, Leningrad Cowboys, Eternal Tears of Sorrow, Ismo Alanko, Hanoi Rocks, Apocalyptica, Waltari, J. Karjalainen, Eppu Normaali and Don Huonot—the names are as interesting as their music. Surprising as it may seem, even popular heavy metal groups like Amorphis draw on lyrics from the *Kalevala,* which still impacts contemporary Finnish culture.

The performing arts are also popular in Finland, with many dramatic and powerful productions in Helsinki by the Helsinki Philharmonic Orchestra, Finnish National Opera, and the Finnish National Theater. Most productions are in Finnish, but the capital also has a Swedish theater located in the city center where productions are conducted in the Swedish language. The performing arts are not found only in Helsinki. In fact, the country boasts of its almost 30 symphony orchestras and 60 theaters in addition to a number of summer theater troupes.

Other visual arts include architecture, sculpture, and paintings. Today Finland's architecture is world famous. Finnish architects like Eliel Saarinen, designer of the beautiful Helsinki Central Railway Station, have won numerous international awards for their work. Wäinö Aaltonen was a world-renowned modernist and nationalist sculptor from Finland who created sculptures of famous Finns like composer Jean Sibelius and distance runner Paavo Nurmi. Finnish artists like Albert Edelfelt, Hugo Simberg, Helene Schjerfbeck, and Akseli Gallen-Kallela have also flourished and are widely recognized outside of Finland.

The arts have remained very strong in Finland over the past centuries and still retain many traits of the distant past. National interests and works like the *Kalevala* remain popular and influence contemporary works. The landscape and Finnish folk heritage also are widely reflected in the works of contemporary Finns. Their love of the land and their culture is reflected in music, literature, visual performances, and by artists and sculptures. Thus, the strong Finnish character is very alive today in the country's arts.

Language

Finland has two official languages, Finnish and Swedish. The Finnish language is included in the languages referred to as Finno-Ugric, whereas Swedish is a Germanic tongue. The Finno-Ugric languages exist today primarily in northeastern Europe and Russia. Only 5.6 percent of the population speaks Swedish today; Finnish, by far, is the dominant language of government and daily life. Other smaller languages also exist in the country, and the most important are Russian and Sami.

Finland's constitution charges the government with assisting in preserving the Sami language.

The Finnish language is phonetic and is spoken by 92 percent of the population. The words in the language are gender nonspecific, as terms refer to both men and women. Words are also frequently very long when compared with other languages because of the linguistic structure used. According to Ville Koskivaara, the longest Finnish word is epäjärjestelmällistyttämättömyydellänsäkään, which is also sometimes spelled epäjärjestelmällistyttämättömyydelläänsäkään. In either case, the word is very long and also very difficult to understand in English. Koskivaara defines it as "even with its quality of not being possible to be made irrational." Finnish also doesn't use articles such as "a" or "the," and it does not have a verb similar to the meaning of "to have."

Finns have borrowed many words from other languages, such as English, German, Swedish, and Slavic languages. These words have been integrated into Finnish and are mixed with traditional Finnish words in daily conversations. In addition, languages like Sami have also borrowed words from Finnish, as the daily languages are fluid and changing with the times to reflect new ideas, objects, and trends. Finnish has also affected other languages that have borrowed words. The Finnish word *sauna*, for example, is used in Canada, the United States, and much of the rest of the world.

Finnish immigrants brought many words to the Western world, creating a blend of Finnish and English language that many have dubbed "Finglish." As a result of television, the Internet, and other media and communications systems, many English words are being adopted. Finnish linguists are concerned about the impact of this, because English has become the language of international business. Even Finland's communications giant, Nokia, has adopted English as the company's official language to stay competitive in the global business environment.

Religion

Visitors to Finland today will see churches and cathedrals scattered across this Nordic country. As in most European nations, Finns have the right to religious freedom, but they often practice it in ways that are somewhat unusual. As we discovered in examining Finland's history, for centuries the country was split between the Orthodox and Catholic faiths. Shortly after Martin Luther, with Mikael Agricola leading the way in Finland, the Lutheran church soon dominated the country. Today, that faith remains overwhelmingly dominant, as nearly 83 percent of Finns claim ties to the Evangelical Lutheran Church. Despite this, it may seem strange that most don't attend services. Only 50 percent attend church even once a year, and a scant 6 percent of the population goes to church at least once a month.

These data indicate that many Finns seem to have a personal and private relationship with their faith, but do not believe as much in public displays. The exceptions to this are the primary events in the life of a Christian, like baptism, marriage, and death rituals. For example, Finnish surveys reveal that 87 percent of Finns are baptized after birth. Over two-thirds get married in church, and a staggering 98 percent have funerals held in a church. Finns also actively support church-sponsored activities in child care, schooling, social welfare, and assistance for the elderly. Thus, the church has many important roles in Finnish society, but in different ways from most churches in the United States and Canada.

Other religions are also present in Finland, but they are much smaller than the Evangelical Lutheran Church. Orthodox Christianity, a remnant of Russia's influence, is practiced by 1.1 percent of the population, about 60,000 people. The patriarchate of Constantinople in Turkey has jurisdiction over the Orthodox Church in Finland, much like the pope in Rome has jurisdiction over Catholics around the world. Other Christian churches also claim about 1.1 percent of the population as members. These include an array of churches including Pentecostal, Roman

The world's largest snow castle can be found in the port town of Kemi in northern Finland. The castle has restaurants, an art gallery, a hotel, and a chapel *(above)*. Many of its furnishings and its decorations are made entirely of ice, and religious services and marriage ceremonies are popular events. Come spring, the snow castle will melt into the sea and be rebuilt the following winter.

Catholic, Jehovah's Witnesses, and Mormons. The country also has an increasing Muslim population. In addition to the Tartars, Finland's first Muslims, many others have immigrated to the country in recent years as workers. Today, Finland's Muslim population is estimated to number between 10,000 and 30,000. The remaining Finns, about 15.1 percent of the population, do not have religious ties to any church.

With its religious heritage, Finland has a number of interesting and notable churches. The Temppeliaukio (Rock) Church in Helsinki was created inside a rock and has a rock altar. Helsinki also has the Helsinki Cathedral, a church built in the mid-nineteenth century, which is very popular with tourists. A third important structure is Turku Cathedral, which is located in the city of Turku on the southwest coast. The cathedral dates back to 1300 and is considered to be the mother church of Finland's Lutheran faith. Today, it serves as the official seat of the archbishop of Finland. After surviving wars and terrible fire, the cathedral has been renovated many times; the last major work took place in 1979. In 2000, Turku Cathedral celebrated its seven-hundredth anniversary.

Finnish Foods

Most Finns eat three meals a day, and some of the traditions of hunting and fishing carry over to today's dinner table. Regional differences are also evident. For example, meat and fish are more evident in western Finland, whereas lighter foods like vegetables and wild mushrooms are favored more in the east. Finnish food favorites include dishes such as cabbage rolls, cold and smoked fish, pickled herring, Karelian hot pot stew, Finnish meatballs, and sausage. Wild game like moose, reindeer, rabbit, duck, and grouse are popular, especially with families who hunt and fish. These leaner meats are also becoming more popular in recent years because of health considerations. Finns eat traditional meats like beef, pork, and chicken, but sausages of many kinds remain a favorite. Sausages range from blood sausage to the city of Turku's saltwater sausage that is also called raisin sausage. Milk, coffee, and alcoholic beverages are all popular drinks.

Finland also grows a lot of berries that add variety to meals. They include lingonberry, cranberry, crowberry, strawberry, raspberry, cloudberry, and the very popular blueberry, which is valued because of its positive impact on health. The berries are mostly used for jams, fruit soups, and desserts; some are also used as sauces for meats and fish. Golden cloudberry is a favorite dessert, but since the cloudberry is one of the world's most expensive berries, it is rarely served.

Many new foods have also been introduced to Finland in recent decades. Today, international foods like pizza, hot dogs, hamburgers, and pasta dishes are now easily found in Helsinki and other cities. The modern Finn diet has also become more health conscious. Even the traditional Finnish sausage now substitutes healthier fats for the animal fats that were traditionally used. Lighter meals are also more evident, and fruits and vegetables are now available throughout the year. This is a major change in recent years, as traditional meals were often dependent on seasonal harvests. Today, Finns enjoy fresh harvests from across the world and year-round because of their modern and efficient transportation systems.

Even though French president Jacques Chirac and Italian prime minister Silvio Berlusconi severely criticized Finnish food early in the twenty-first century, most people find it very pleasing and satisfying. The use of pure and natural ingredients adds to the appeal and taste of Finnish cuisine. Today's visitors have a great variety of outstanding options when dining in the country.

A LOOK BACK AT FINLAND'S PEOPLE

Finns have always been a hearty and resilient people, and they have had to be. Located in a remote area of the world with a challenging climate and sometimes difficult neighbors, their culture has helped them not only to survive, but also to enjoy life. Life today is very good for most Finns, but it is not perfect. Alcoholism and suicides remain major social issues. Alcohol consumption is still among the highest in the world, despite government efforts to curtail the problem.

Finland has been a very progressive country in terms of promoting gender equality. As one of the world's first countries to grant women the right to vote, Finland has many women in key leadership positions today. A woman is president today. However, there remains room for improvement, as Finnish women still earn about 20 percent less than their male counterparts. This problem is similar to that in the United States and many other countries. Despite the considerable progress thus far, additional work remains to be done.

While there is little diversity in religion and ethnicity in Finland, there are still distinct minority groups. These groups practice many of their traditional beliefs and add immensely to the Finnish culture as a whole. The minority cultures, languages, and religions are all protected by Finland's constitution. Discussion of the country's political dimensions in the following chapter will help to further your understanding of the relationships that exist between Finns and their government.

CHAPTER

6

Government and Politics

In 2006, Finland handed out a world-record fine for a speeding ticket. A son of Finland's sausage king, Jussi Salonja, was picked up for driving 50 miles (80 kilometers) per hour in a 25 mph (40 km/h) zone in downtown Helsinki. For this offense, the no-nonsense Finns convicted Salonja with a law that is particularly harsh because it bases fines on a person's wealth and income rather than a set rate. This meant that the multimillionaire sausage empire heir was fined a whopping 170,000 euros or $217,000 in U.S. dollars!

Laws and governments are elements that come out of a country's culture and heritage. Mores (social customs) and traditions usually serve as a foundation for the laws that are developed by a country's government. With the exception of fancy cars, Finns are rather modest about their wealth. Since the country is the only one in Europe that never had a king or aristocracy of its own, Finns tend to be quite private about their assets. For example, Finland's sausage king (Jussi's father) lives in a very humble and relatively small ranch-style home in the town of Kouvola, in an average neighborhood. There is one major difference, however. This home contains millions of dollars worth of paintings by the Masters—even on the walls of the garage and above the kitchen sink. A city traffic officer lives across the street in this very average community. The speeding laws in Finland have accommodated disparities in income so as to discourage all speeders, regardless of their power and wealth.

Finland is also a culture that values honesty. This trait extends to the government and society as a whole. Finns can be proud that their country consistently ranks as one of the least corrupt in the world, according to Transparency International. Bribery and other forms of corruption virtually do not exist. Lack of corruption and a liberal social welfare system are key factors in keeping poverty low, which makes the Finns and their government very proud. Thus, the probability of a wealthy person bribing a police officer to get out of a ticket is not likely to happen in Finland.

The example of the speeding ticket also demonstrates that the Finns go their own way when it comes to governance. Citizens greatly value their country and their democratic society. Their struggle for independence, which was achieved in 1917, has been tattooed on the souls of Finland's citizens. As Russia deteriorated and Finland's independence became assured, the Finns first argued about whether to have a monarchy or a republic. In 1919, the first Finnish constitution was adopted and used until 2000. During the first constitution, the Finns' determined defiance of the Soviet Union during World War II further shaped the hearty civic attitude and independence that is exhibited by Finns today.

WHY GOVERNMENT?

Governments are instituted by citizens to provide order in societies and to do things collectively that individuals are incapable of doing alone. For example, governments provide safety, health, education, roads, military, foreign relations, and quality standards. They also preserve individual rights and provide other key functions. James Madison, American president and political thinker, wrote in *The Federalist No. 51*: "If men were angels, no government would be necessary." With this paper, Madison also cautioned societies to limit powers within government. The phrase "absolute power corrupts absolutely" seems to be true about human behavior. Thus, this characteristic is usually tempered in democratic governments by checks and balances instituted between government offices and branches of government. As a republic, Finland has had to wrestle with these questions when creating the new constitution that was adopted on March 1, 2000.

Government consists of the formal institutions a society has conferred with the authority to create and implement laws, rules, and policies that govern a society. Institutions can be courts, legislative bodies, ministries, a president, municipal councils, or other bodies that carry out the functions of government. Politics is the process used in a country to reach decisions. In a democracy, this process includes all citizens and groups who are eligible and who choose to participate. The political parties that provide different views regarding the roles of government and existing and pending public policies are a key factor in politics.

In democratic societies, the rule of law prevails over the rule of man. This means that all citizens, even the president, are subject to the laws of the country. In situations where the rule of man exists, as in North Korea, some people are above the law and not held accountable. Usually, the rule of man exists in dictatorships where the power of the leader(s) or the wealthy is more important than the laws of the land. In societies where there is the rule of law, citizens all enjoy equal protection under the law. This does not exist in societies where the rule of man prevails. The Finnish sausage king heir obviously lives in a society where the rule of law prevails.

FINLAND'S CONSTITUTION AND BRANCHES OF GOVERNMENT

Finland's government is established by the constitution. The constitution is the highest law in the country, as it is in other democratic countries where the rule of law prevails. Finland's new constitution was adopted in 2000 and replaced the earlier 1919 constitution. Thus, the document is very modern when compared to the constitution of the United States, which is over two centuries old. The new constitution establishes the primary institutions and processes of the Finnish government.

Three branches of government are created by the constitution. First is the executive branch, which is headed by the president, but with some duties also specified for the prime minister. Second is the legislative branch. In Finland the unicameral parliament is called the Eduskunta. Unicameral means that the legislative branch has only one house. This is different from Canada or the United States, in which (with the exception of Nebraska) there are bicameral legislatures, or two houses. The legislative branch is primarily responsible for making public policy. The third arm of government is the judicial branch. This is the court system, which is charged with interpreting the constitution and other laws. The highest court in Finland is the Supreme Court, which in Finnish is called the Korkein Oikeus.

Finland's constitution also establishes other key elements that are at the highest level of law. These include such things as establishing Finland's land area, rule of law, citizens' rights and freedoms, citizenship, international relations, and national defense. The following sections examine the branches of government and other parts of the constitution that impact and protect citizens in the country.

The Executive Branch

The president is the chief of state in Finland, and the prime minister is the head of government. This means that the president is the symbol of the country and is responsible for many executive functions related to appointments and foreign relations. The president is also the commander-in-chief of the armed forces, much like the president in the United States, who also has this responsibility. Other duties of the president include being able to order early parliamentary elections, appointing ministers and other high officials, signing and putting new laws into action, and pardoning criminals. As chief of state, the president can bestow titles, medals, and awards on behalf of the country. The president also appoints the governor to the autonomous Aland Islands. A final, but most important, authority is the president's emergency powers in times of crisis.

Who can become president in Finland? The criteria are actually quite simple in that the president must be native born and elected by a majority of the popular vote. If there are more than two candidates and no candidate receives more than 50 percent of the vote, a second election is held between the top two candidates in the first presidential election. Presidents may serve no more than two six-year terms. Finland's constitution does not provide for a vice president. Thus, if the position of president becomes vacant, an election for a new president will be held as soon as possible.

Although the president serves as the chief of state, the prime minister is actually responsible for the day-to-day executive management of Finland's national government. If the president is out of the country or not able to fulfill his or her responsibilities, the prime minister steps in to perform these duties. More responsibilities of the prime minister are described in the next section.

The Eduskunta

The constitution creates the unicameral Eduskunta that has 200 members. Members are elected for terms of four years with elections held in March 2007, 2011, 2015, and so on thereafter. Members of parliament (MP) are elected by a secret ballot that is cast by Finnish citizens who are 18 or older. These members are elected proportionally from districts that are established across the country. Each of these districts has a select number of MP seats that are filled in elections. The Aland Islands are also allowed to elect one MP to represent them.

Political parties nominate the candidates for the Eduskunta. The major political parties in Finland with the number of seats held in late 2006 include the Center Party (55 seats); Social Democratic Party (53); National Coalition Party (40); Left Wing Alliance (19); Green League (14); Swedish People's Party (8); Christian Democrats (7); True Finns (3); and the Aland representative (1). It takes a majority to form a government; because Finland has a multiparty system, it is usually impossible for one party to create a government. Thus, coalitions are formed to establish a government. For example, in 2003, the Center, Social Democratic, and Swedish People's parties formed a ruling coalition. In the elections for the Eduskunta in March 2007, a new, more conservative coalition than that of 2003 was formed among four political parties. These included the National Coalition Party with 50 seats, the Center Party with 51 seats, the Green League with 15 seats, and the Swedish People's Party with 9 seats. For the first time since 1995, the Social Democratic Party with 45 seats was left out of the ruling coalition and instead headed the opposition.

Any citizen can run for a seat in parliament, except for citizens in the military and people who hold select government positions, like justices of the Supreme Court, the president, or the prosecutor-general. If an MP is serving in the European Parliament, they are not able to serve in the Finnish Eduskunta. Instead, their deputy serves in their place.

Finland prides itself on its high standards of equality. Finnish women were the first in Europe to exercise the right to vote and to have their eligibility for office recognized. Here, voters in Helsinki cast their ballots in the 2007 legislative elections.

The Eduskunta elects the prime minister, who is then formally appointed by the president. The prime minister directs the activities and work of the government and chairs meetings of the ministers. The prime minister also has primary responsibility for European Union issues. Other ministers, who head various departments, are appointed by the president. Examples of departments in Finland's government include ministries for

Foreign Affairs, Defense, Education, Finance, Interior, Labor, Justice, Transport and Communications, Interior, and the Environment. Each of these departments is charged with managing the ongoing government activities in the designated area of responsibility. They are also responsible for implementing new directions and policies that the government has established.

The primary responsibility of the Eduskunta is to put forward public policy initiatives that may be considered by the body and enacted into law. These may include budget matters, along with other laws necessary to advance the ruling coalition's agenda for the government and the country. As the legislative branch of government for Finland, the Eduskunta has a number of committees that investigate and forward bills to the entire body for consideration. Acts passed by the Eduskunta are passed on to the president, who has three months to confirm or reject the proposed law. If the president does not confirm the law, it is sent back to the Eduskunta for further consideration. The Eduskunta can pass a law without the president's confirmation by simply passing the bill a second time. This feature allows for each of these two parts of government to check each other.

Finland's parliament also has the power to accept or reject treaties. Another very important power is the Eduskunta's ability to determine the budget and taxes. In addition, as a member of the European Union, the Eduskunta considers and acts upon proposals from the European Commission.

Finland's Court System

The Finnish court system is responsible for interpreting the laws and fairly determining guilt or responsibility in court cases brought before them. The country has a long record of judicial fairness and independence from outside influences. This is important in the effort to retain the rule of law that holds even public officials accountable for following the country's laws.

The constitution provides for three levels of courts. The highest is the Supreme Court, which is called the Korkein Oikeus. Below this body are the Courts of Appeal and District Courts. Other courts are also created by the constitution for special purposes, like the High Court of Impeachment, or the Insurance Court.

The Korkein Oikeus is the last court of appeal for civil and criminal cases in the country, as there is no higher court. This court has a presiding judge called the president, and the court must have 15 or more members (in 2007, the court had 18 members). The president of the country appoints judges on the Korkein Oikeus, and they may serve until they are 68 years old. They may also retire early, or be removed by an impeachment process.

There are six courts of appeal in the country that serve to take cases that are appealed and accepted from district courts. These courts are located in major cities including Turku, Helsinki, Kouvola, and Vaasa, and they usually receive cases in which the decisions of a district court are disputed by one of the original parties.

Sixty-one district courts exist in Finland, and they rule on both civil and criminal cases. Criminal cases are ones like the earlier-mentioned speeding case, where convicted individuals can receive fines or time in jail. Civil cases are usually between two or more parties where compensation or relief is sought. Examples of civil cases are divorces, lawsuits, or child custody disputes.

PROVINCIAL AND LOCAL GOVERNMENTS

Finland also has local governments that administer municipalities and political subdivisions of the country. For example, just as there are states in the United States or provinces in Canada, Finland has five provinces and Swedish-speaking Aland, which is a self-ruled province. The provinces have a governor as the chief executive, as well as provincial boards that are responsible to the national Ministry of the Interior. Below the provinces are the municipalities and other local areas that are governed by elected councils. Finland has more than 400 local governments.

The constitution allows local governments to raise money by taxes so that they can meet their responsibilities, which are very important to citizens. These include a wide variety of activities, like building roads, operating schools, and conducting adult education programs. They also provide day care for children, supervision of land use, promotion of business, maintenance of health and welfare systems, and the management of water use and waste disposal. A municipal council will have at least seven elected members. Below the council, there are municipal employees who carry on the daily activities required of local governments. These individuals serve under the direction of the elected body. Including all local governments, municipal councils employ about one-fifth of Finland's workforce.

POLITICAL PARTIES

When a political system has proportional representation assigned to political parties after elections, it is almost certain that there will be multiple political parties that represent many viewpoints. This is very true in Finland where the multiparty system affords numerous political perspectives, and considerably different from the United States, where only two major political parties prevail.

Finland's larger political parties include the Social Democratic Party of Finland (SDP), the Center Party (Keskusta), and the conservative National Coalition. Each of these parties usually receives between 20 and 30 percent of the vote in elections. The SDP mainly represents the interests of working people, while the Center Party is a voice for rural interests. The conservatives tend to draw their support from the business community and professionals.

Pictured here is an electoral poster for the Social Democratic Party (SDP). With approximately 59,000 members, the SDP is one of the most influential political parties in Finland. However, in the 2007 parliamentary election, the SDP lost 8 seats and finished in third place for the first time since 1962.

Smaller political parties also represent other, more narrow, interests. These parties include the Left Wing Alliance, Green League, Swedish People's Party, Christian Democrats, Communists, and the True Finns. The Communist party was legalized in 1944, but it has had little support and usually falls within the Left Wing Alliance.

Coalition governments are formed out of necessity because of the numerous political parties. To accomplish this, various political parties agree to work together to form a coalition that will rule the government. Each of the parties is then given ministries to lead, with the strongest parties holding the most important and greatest number of ministries.

THE ROLE OF CITIZENS

The Finnish constitution protects citizens in the country by ensuring important rights and freedoms. Many of these protections are similar to provisions in the United Nation's Declaration of Human Rights and to those provided in other modern democracies. These rights include:

- Equality
- The right to life, personal liberty, and integrity
- Freedom of movement
- The right to privacy
- Freedom of religion and conscience
- Freedom of expression and right of access to information
- Freedom of assembly and freedom of association
- Electoral and participatory rights
- Protection of property
- Educational rights
- Right to one's language and culture
- The right to work and the freedom to engage in commercial activity
- The right to social security
- Protection under the law

The government has the primary responsibility for making certain that citizens' rights are protected. Finland has a strong record in the area of human rights and, if needed, even allows citizens to appeal violations to international bodies outside the country to seek justice.

WOMEN IN GOVERNMENT

Tarja Halonen is the first woman president of Finland. She was elected in 2000 and was reelected to a second term in 2006 as a member of the Finnish Social Democratic Party. Women are well represented in parliament, with 42 percent of the members in 2007. They also are active in the cabinet with 12 out of 20 ministries led by women in the 2007 parliament. This is the highest percentage of women in governmental leadership positions in the world. Thus, Finland is much more advanced than the United States, Canada, and many other countries in terms of having women equitably in leadership positions.

This is also true of Finnish society where women and minorities are guaranteed equality. Section 6 of the constitution states that "Everyone is equal before the law." The constitution also states that equality extends to activities in society including pay and employment. This progressive attitude has allowed Finnish women to play an active role in government, business, and society as a whole.

FOREIGN POLICY

For much of the twentieth century, Finland was trying to keep the Soviet Union at bay. This huge neighbor with its world-class military has posed a continual threat to the feisty Finns. Today, relations with Russia have improved, so Finns have less to be concerned about on this front for a number of reasons. One was Finland's continuing policy of neutrality since World War II, which has made Finland less of a threat to Russia and has worked well for the Finns. Another is that Finland maintains a small military that is defensive in nature. The country's forces may only participate in conflicts if they are sanctioned by the United Nations or the Organization for Security and Co-operation in Europe (OSCE). However, even as a neutral nation, much of the country's economy and political connections are linked with the West.

As an example, Finland became an active member of the European Union (EU) in 1995. Previously, this may have been a threat to the Soviet Union, but after the fall of the communist regime, Finland has been freer to pursue the course it wants without posing a threat to Russia.

The EU has created an amazing transformation in Europe since the mid-twentieth century. For centuries, European countries struggled for independence and advantages over their neighbors. Countless wars were fought to establish supremacy or independence. Borders were uncertain as armies trudged over them to conquer others.

Today, Europe has a new dynamic wave washing over the countries in the region. This EU wave has affected governments, economies, and cultures. Almost all EU countries have voluntarily given up their national currencies, and they allow workers to move freely between European labor markets, making it much easier for people to cross borders. As a result, ideas, goods, services, and many other aspects of culture are being exchanged and assimilated. Thus, the EU has greatly changed Europe, and the diverse cultures that have existed for thousands of years are now impacted by other cultures in the EU. Finland is no exception.

Finland is also an active player on the world stage in other ways. The country is a member of numerous international organizations including the United Nations (UN), International Monetary Fund (IMF), Interpol, World Trade Organization (WTO), Arctic Council, General Agreement on Tariffs and Trade (GATT), the Council of Europe, and many others. Finland has also signed on to many international agreements and treaties on a wide variety of issues. They include air pollution, biodiversity, climate change, endangered species, desertification, hazardous waste, ozone depletion, marine dumping, wetlands, and whaling.

The political directions of the country also color the nation's economic prospects. Governments play an extensive role in helping or hindering the economy of a country. Finland's government is no exception to this rule. Thus, the country's vital economic prospects and scenarios will be investigated in the next chapter.

7

Finland:
An Economic
Powerhouse

For centuries, Finland existed as a distant outpost of humankind. Life in that era was extremely difficult and most Finns
lived on a survival basis. The incredibly hostile cold winter
environment made life fragile, as satisfying basic needs like food,
clothing, and shelter demanded great efforts in order to survive. The
country's past also showed that it moved from being on the outside
to being in the middle of major conflicts between Sweden and Russia. Later, during the Cold War, Finland was caught in a difficult
position between the Soviet Union and the West. How has Finland's
heritage shaped the country's economic landscape? Does the country exist today in an economic dead zone, a virtual political purga-
tory in between Russia and the West? Have the Finns figured out
ways not only to survive, but to prosper, in today's global economy?
We will examine the answers to these questions and others in this
chapter.

Geographers are very interested in the spatial organization, distribution, and location of economic activities. In early Finland, economic activity was simple as people hunted, gathered, and fished for their food. They lived a subsistence lifestyle and fought to protect themselves from the environment and other dangers. When people live at subsistence levels, it means that they are barely surviving. This characterized the life of Finland's peoples for most of their history.

Today, Finland is markedly different in terms of its economic geography. A vibrant economy has allowed the Finns to have the eleventh highest per-capita Gross Domestic Product (GDP) in the world. The 2006 edition of the World Bank Development Indicators reported this ranking in 2006, noting that the average per-capita GDP was US$37,460 per year. This also represented an increase of more than $4,500 from the data of the previous year for the country. In contrast, the average GDP for the United States was ranked sixth and Canada nineteenth. Thus, it appears that Finland has moved from subsistence to prosperity. What has contributed to the success of the Finns? What drives their economy, and what industries have prospered to generate the country's wealth? For the answers to these questions and others, further investigation is required.

NATURAL RESOURCES

Finland has a number of natural resources that have assisted in the country's economic development. Among these are iron ore, copper, lead, zinc, chromite, nickel, gold, silver, and limestone. The country also has abundant forest resources. The sawmill and paper industries are spin-offs of the country's timber industry. They remain strong contributors to the Finns' economy, while many of the country's formerly rich mineral deposits are now depleted. Instead, Finland has mined the fertile minds of the Finnish people, whose ingenuity has spawned various industries and other economic developments.

With fewer natural resources, recent efforts have been made to develop sustainable resources for the country; they would be renewable and include such things as recycling paper and other waste, and reusing materials. It also includes sustainable energy produced with biofuels, as well as hydroelectric and wind-generated power. The Finns are a leading nation and quite strict in terms of environmental protection of basic natural resources like the air, land, and water.

Even though the Finns are protective of their environment, they also are pragmatic. Mining efforts still exist in the country today. Gold, copper, and nickel are a few of the mineral industries active in Finland. New mineral areas are still being explored, as promising deposits of scarce commodities like platinum and uranium have been found in Finland. Platinum deposits have been located near the Arctic Circle in Lapland, while uranium deposits have been found in the north, south, and east. The development of the uranium may be slow, if it even happens, because local citizens have resisted uranium mining. Additionally, in early 2007, Finland's Ministry of Trade and Industry refused requests to mine uranium in Lapland, or in the south near Helsinki. Since Finland has an extensive nuclear power program, the temptation to mine uranium may increase as global supplies dwindle.

Timber remains Finland's most important natural resource. The country has become exceedingly efficient in using its timber; nothing is wasted in adding value to the raw material: wood. Even sawdust and wood chips are used to make pulp and chipboard. The Finns' pulp industry is very advanced and makes high-quality papers. Woodworking is still an active industry, and Finland manufactures many woodworking and paper-producing machines. In fact, the Finnish company called Metso is the world's leading producer of machines that make paper.

Although Finland is dependent on its forests for its economic welfare, environmental groups are concerned that the wood-processing industry is threatening the biodiversity of ancient forests and local plants and animals. The Finnish government has set aside about 10 percent of its forests for biodiversity conservation and recreational purposes.

AGRICULTURE

Located between 60 degrees and 70 degrees north latitude, a position comparable to that of Alaska, Finland has a climate that is ill-suited for most agriculture. Add to this poor soil, and agriculture has never been an important contributor to the country's economy. Global climate changes may temporarily create more suitable climatic conditions. Snowless winters, for example, have become more common in southern Finland. The leading Finnish contributor to the Intergovernmental Panel on Climate Change (IPCC) has projected that if the trend continues, temperatures in Finland will increase by 2.7°F to 16.2°F (1.5°C to 9°C) within a century.

Although the Finns have a short growing season, they have a long growing day because of their location in the far north. This means that parts of the country will receive 18 or more hours of daylight in the summer with total daylight poleward of the Arctic Circle. Most of the agricultural sector is located in the southwestern region of the country. Crops include barley, oats, wheat, sugar beets, and potatoes. Finns raise animals such as dairy cattle, and they farm fish.

Agriculture makes up less than 3 percent of the country's GDP, but it employs 4.4 percent of the population. While the industry is not as important as others in the country, the Finns have the most productive agriculture sector of any country located in the far north.

MANUFACTURING

In the past, wood and paper products comprised much of Finland's manufacturing sector. Today, however, advanced technologies have helped the country's economy to expand even faster. The Finns have the ability to adapt to changing circumstances, perhaps as a result of living in a hostile environment for centuries. The example of global giant Nokia will assist in explaining this phenomenon.

When people think of Nokia, they think of the immense modern global corporation that develops and manufactures high-quality cell phones. While true, this is only a part of their story. The company actually started as a pulp mill on the Tammerkoski Rapids in southwestern Finland in 1865, over

140 years ago. Over its history, the company has moved from manufacturing toilet paper and paper pulp to cell phones. Are there any connections between these industries? According to Nokia there are, as they consider paper to be the original communication system. After pulp, the company started a cable company and in 1960 ventured into electronics. The company then thrust itself into the emerging mobile phone market and by 1998 was the world's leader in this area. Incredibly, Nokia exceeded total sales of nearly one billion mobile phones in 2005. Today the company has factories in Romania, China, Mexico, India, Hungary, Germany, and, of course, back home in Finland. However, high labor costs in Finland have necessitated that Nokia produce phones in countries with lower labor costs to compete in the global marketplace. From paper pulp to next-generation mobile phones, Nokia has adapted to the changing global marketplace.

Another impact of Nokia is the wealth it has created. Obviously, Finnish workers have benefited from the good jobs at Nokia, but hundreds of investors have also become millionaires by owning the company's stock. How large is Nokia's economic influence in Finland? In 2007, the company had an annual budget that exceeded the national government's budget. Nokia's impact also reaches to other manufacturers, since many other companies supply parts and equipment to the global giant. The reach of the world's largest mobile communications company is global, and its effect on Finland's economy is huge. Other aspects of Finnish life are affected; the country even holds an annual Mobile-Phone-Throwing World Championship in the city of Savolinna. Naturally a Finn, named Lassi Etelatalo, won the event with a throw of 291.991 feet (89 meters). The phone thrown? A Nokia, of course!

Nokia is not the only high-tech manufacturing concern in the economy. New efforts in nanotechnology have helped this industry boom in Finland. More than 125 companies were reported as working with nanotechnology in 2006, which is more than double the number that existed only two years earlier (61 companies). Most of these innovative efforts are in the areas of health care, food, and chemicals.

Traditional industries also remain strong, as the country recorded record production of pulp, paperboard, and paper in 2006 with an incredible increase of 14 percent over the previous year. Other manufacturing is important in industries like metals and metal products, next-generation electronics, machinery and scientific instruments, shipbuilding, foodstuffs, chemicals, textiles, and clothing. As noted earlier, it is more difficult for the Finns in these traditional industries, as labor costs are very high. Even though the country manufactures clothing, it produces only about 10 percent of the country's needs, and the clothing produced is for high-end Finnish designers like Luhta and Marimekko. Thus, the Finnish economy manufactures items ranging from cruise ships and icebreakers to the tiny products of nanotechnology. High technology has become a vitally important element for the Finns, as they have readily adapted to globalization and the world's rapidly evolving economy.

TOURISM

Tourism is a relatively new industry in Finland. Long viewed by others as locked in the frigid north, Finland's changing climate and strong global presence is now attracting visitors in unprecedented numbers. Tourism can be very valuable to an economy, since it usually has little negative impact on the environment and can create a lot of jobs. Tourists need lodging, transportation, food, and things to do when they are visiting. All of these aspects of tourism create jobs in Finland in either the public or private sectors.

Where do Finland's tourists come from? Increasingly, the answer to this question is from all around the world, as well as from Finland itself. Tourists are domestic and from other countries, and both add to the nation's economy. In 2004, the Ministry of Trade and Industry reported that tourism contributed more than 9 billion euros to the country's economy. Most of this money, 73 percent, came from domestic tourists, and international guests comprised the other 27 percent. International tourists have rapidly increased in recent years, as well; the ministry reports that these tourists created nearly 60,000 jobs in 2004.

In the competitive international tourism industry, it is important to examine the advantages Finland has in tourism when compared to other countries. According to the London-based World Travel & Tourism Council (WTTC), Finland has competitive advantages in three key areas: the country's environment (ranked third in this category), human resources (also ranked third), and social factors like the country's status as the least corrupt country in the world. With these key advantages and interesting sights, Finland's foreign tourists are increasing. For example, tourists from India increased 45 percent from 2005 to 2006, and Chinese tourists increased by 30 percent at the same time. Over the Christmas and New Year's holidays in 2006–2007, 80,000 Russian tourists flooded into Finland, a 60 percent increase over the prior holiday season. Why do they come? Helsinki, Lapland, shopping, and Santa Claus are some of the reasons. Others are absolutely Finnwacky!

There are over 40 Finnwacky events in Finland each year. These include a range of events like the previously mentioned Mobile-Phone-Throwing World Championship and a lot more. Perhaps visitors would like to participate in the Wife-Carrying World Championship, Air Guitar Contest, Milking-Stool-Throwing Contest, Mosquito Swatting, Snowshoe football, Sleepyhead Day, or the World Swamp Football championship. Serious sauna competition also exists with the World Sauna Championship, where participants come from around the world and start in water at 230°F (110°C). The temperature then rises every 30 seconds until the last man and woman remain. Hot competition for both Finns and tourists! Oddball events aren't the only attractions in Finland. Perhaps you'd like

Beautiful scenery, peacefulness, and clean air are just a few reasons why Finland is attracting visitors in increasingly large numbers. Winter is an ideal time to visit, with hundreds of thousands of tourists arriving for Christmas festivities and winter sports such as skiing, dog sledding, and touring by snowmobile.

to stay at the newly opened Hotel Katajanokka in Helsinki, which was a Finnish prison from the nineteenth century until 2002. Finnwacky indeed!

TRANSPORTATION

Transportation systems are the key connectors for human and economic activity. They allow people, goods, and services to move between locations. Modern global economies not only must have a strong transportation infrastructure (within the country), but also connections to key suppliers and markets around the world. With Finland's location intersecting with the Arctic Circle, the country has had challenges that many other warmer countries would not face.

Paved highways and other improved roads are the most important form of transportation today in the country. Cities are connected by a well-developed road system that allows people and goods to move efficiently. The country has 48,584.39 total miles of roads (78,189 kilometers), about 65 percent of which are paved. First-rate high-speed motorways (European term for roads like interstate highways in the United States) connect major cities. The northernmost motorway in the world is in Lapland and connects the cities of Kemi and Tornio.

Trains offer another land-based form of transportation, since the Finnish rail system has 3,567.66 miles (5,741 kilometers) of track. Trains transport about one-fourth of the goods moved in the country, and this amount is increasing each year as energy prices rise. Nearly 60 million passengers also took trains in 2003 with this amount increasing about one percent every year.

Airports provide another important piece of Finland's transportation infrastructure. Because of Finland's distance from many other major European cities, airports provide a speedy transportation alternative for people and goods. Fourteen percent of Finland's exports travel by air, and this decade more than 13 million people are using the country's airports each year, with their numbers increasing annually. There are 148 airports in the country, and 76 of these have paved runways. Many remote Finnish communities depend upon air transportation, especially in winter, as their main form of travel and for delivery of goods.

Helsinki is home to Helsinki-Vantaa International Airport, the country's largest. The airport is very popular with travelers and has repeatedly ranked among the top-rated airports in the world over the past decade. In 2006 it served over 12 million passengers who could choose from over 25 international and domestic airlines. Finnair, the country's flagship carrier, is based at the airport and connects the country to many other nations throughout the world. From Helsinki, a traveler can fly directly to major cities such as Beijing, Tokyo, Bangkok, London, New York, Shanghai, and Hong Kong. This air link is vitally important in connecting the Finns to trading partners.

The sea provides another important dimension for Finland's transportation system. Ports are located at Hamina, Hanko, Kotka, Naantali, Pori, Porvoo, Raahe, Rauma, and Turku, with the largest port located in Helsinki. The Port of Helsinki serves over 9 million passengers each year and handles over 100 million tons of cargo. Almost all of the cargo is foreign trade. Approximately 90 percent of the country's foreign exports and 70 percent of foreign imports depart or arrive by sea. These factors make the Port of Helsinki the second largest port in Nordic countries. Passenger traffic is daily from Helsinki to Sweden, Estonia, and Germany on ferries. Cruise ships frequently stop in the port and bring travelers from around the world.

The sea is not the only form of water transportation in Finland. Canals, rivers, and lakes form another network for water travel. This system provides the southeastern part of the country with 4,873 miles (7,842 kilometers) of waterways. These waterways are used for passenger traffic, cruises, and the shipping of products to and from rural areas to major ports.

COMMUNICATIONS

Finland is a global giant in communications. In addition to Nokia, the country has embraced other new technologies and systems. For example, according to the Communications Ministry of Finland, 96 percent of all Finns were connected to the Internet in 2007, which made it the most connected country in the world. The number of Finns under the age of 40 using the Internet is 100 percent. The Internet country code for Finland is .fi and in 2006, according to the CIA World Factbook, the country had approximately 1.6 million Internet hosts. The infrastructure for communications is equally impressive, since digital fiber-optic fixed-line networks dominate the country.

Finland is truly a communications colossus today and is actively planning the development and implementation of an online college called Finnish Virtual University (FVU).

Telephones also place the country as a world leader. Although it is hard to believe, the country has more cell phones than it does people! With all of these cell phones, one would imagine that there are few landlines. This would be a mistake: The country has over 2.1 million landlines, or about one for every 2.5 Finns. The postal system is also extremely efficient and trustworthy. Thus, in terms of personal communications, Finland is a modern, high-tech world leader. How about mass communications?

Mass communications includes a variety of media such as television, radio, newspapers, and magazines. According to most current data, the country had 120 television stations in 1999 and 186 FM radio stations in 1998. There is less reliance on AM radio stations in Finland, since there were only two in 1998. Newspapers remain very popular, even with the high Internet usage. Recent National Readership Survey estimates showed that the average Finn older than age 12 reads three newspapers. The country has 53 daily papers, as well as 146 that are published less frequently. Major newspapers include *Helsingin Sanomat* and *Ilta-Sanomat*. Both are read by about a million people. Others with more than 180,000 readers include *Iltalehti, Aamulehti, Maaseudun Tulevaisuus, Turun Sanomat, Kauppalehti, Kaleva, IS Veikkaaja* and *Keskisuomalainen*. The country also has a wide range of magazines that range from entertainment to intellectual, much like other developed countries.

Clearly Finland is an exceptional place for personal and mass communications and information. With this high access to information, it is not surprising that Finns are some of the best educated and most literate people on the planet. This access to information has contributed mightily to Finland's economy and has made the country a twenty-first century communications superpower.

In a relatively short time, Finland has transformed itself from an agricultural economy to a high-tech economy, associated more with mobile phone company Nokia than with timber felling. In fact, all Finnish schools and public libraries are connected to the Internet. Here, a Finnish woman surfs the Internet at a café in Helsinki.

FOREIGN TRADE AND THE EUROPEAN UNION

We have already discovered Finland's transportation and communication connections to the world. This section explores the foreign trade that the country conducts, and later investigates Finland's important and evolving economic involvement in the European Union.

Other than previously discussed Nokia, Finland has a lot to sell to the world. What else does the country export? Major exports include machinery and equipment, electronics, chemicals, metals, timber, dairy products, paper, and pulp. Within these broad categories, a wide variety of things are exported, ranging from eggs and fur to ships and telecommunications equipment. These products are exported to countries around the world; primary export partners in 2005 were Russia (11.2 percent); Sweden (10.7 percent); Germany (10.5 percent); United Kingdom (6.6 percent); United States (6.2 percent); and the Netherlands (4.8 percent).

Imports are also very important to Finland. Some of these are key ingredients for items manufactured in the country, like telecommunications equipment. Others are raw materials that are vital to industrial production and domestic use, such as petroleum. The main imports include foodstuffs, petroleum and petroleum products, chemicals, transportation equipment, iron and steel, machinery, yarn, fabrics, and grains. Major import trading partners in 2005 were Germany (16.2 percent); Sweden (14.1 percent); Russia (13.9 percent); Netherlands (6.2 percent); Denmark (4.6 percent); United Kingdom (4.3 percent); and China (4.2 percent).

The European Union has presented Finland with many new opportunities. The country joined the organization in 1995 and has risen quickly. In fact, a Finn was president of the EU in the second half of 1999 and 2006. A primary goal of the EU is European integration. Economic integration is a major element in this effort and has included a number of steps designed to reduce economic barriers between European countries. Among these is the introduction of the euro, which has replaced the many national currencies that existed just a few years ago. Fees accompanied currency transactions that increased the costs of doing business or simply traveling to a neighboring country. Other economic aspects include the free movement of labor, free trade, and the creation of a single market. The countries also have common agricultural, fisheries, custom duties, and taxation policies.

Today, the EU has taken on many other responsibilities designed to integrate Europe. These include such things as educational, legal, political, cultural, athletic, environmental, and foreign relations activities. A major effort to integrate politically by creating an EU constitution had stalled by mid-2007. Citizen votes against the constitution in France and the

Netherlands have slowed the progress on this front, and diffi-culties in other members also have slowed the effort. Finland's Eduskunta, however, overwhelmingly ratified the EU constitu-tion in December of 2006.

ECONOMIC CHALLENGES

One of Finland's major challenges is to develop energy self-sufficiency. World dependency on oil is costly and cannot be sustained for the long term because of increased demand and dwindling supplies. The Green League, one of the political par-ties in the 2007 elections for the Eduskunta, even advocated an oil-free economy by 2030. To increase power by other means, a sixth nuclear power plant is slated for completion by 2016, and new efforts in biofuels are being initiated along with wind-power generation.

Climate changes also may have a strong impact on the economy of Finland. The warming of the planet may extin-guish species of plants and animals that live in a narrow temperature range. The high-projected temperature change for Finland presents some unknowns that may also harm the economy. At the same time, Finland, with cutting-edge knowl-edge and technology, is helping others to develop advanced environmentally friendly communities in places like Gego, a city near Beijing, China.

Another economic challenge for the Finns is their high labor costs. As a result of the high wages that exist in the coun-try, Finland will continue to outsource production facilities to other countries with lower labor costs. This could also impact the country by causing the unemployment rate to rise.

The fabulous Finns will most likely continue to display their ingenuity and will successfully navigate the foreseeable challenges to their economy. As a communications superpower with both feet firmly planted in the twenty-first century, its fantastic economic future is probable.

8

Finland
Looks Ahead

Finland is an amazing country. Examining the past, the Finns have had to overcome numerous challenges and obstacles, which has repeatedly demonstrated the resilience and heartiness of the Finnish people.

First was the country's location and natural environment, which presented conditions that made living a daily struggle. Cast in a very remote and northerly location with lands between 60 degrees and 70 degrees north latitude, the environment was hardly the best for human habitation. Food, clothing, and shelter were life-and-death needs on a daily basis during the cold winter months, which in Lapland are about 200 days long. In contrast, the south has about 100 days of winter. Harsh winter conditions present the most northern points in Finland with 51 consecutive days of darkness. Even the warmer south gets only six hours of daylight in the time around the winter solstice (December 21). The daylight winter conditions of southern Finland are very similar to the northern U.S. city of Anchorage in Alaska.

Summers reward winter-weary Finns by providing 24 hours of daylight for as much as 73 days in the far north and 19 hours of daylight in the south. Surviving the country's harsh winters was only the first major challenge for the Finns.

Another major challenge was the fact that Finland frequently found itself trapped in major historical struggles. At times the issue was religion, as the country was caught between the Orthodox and Catholic churches. At other times, Finland was the primary battlefield in the struggles between its powerful neighbors to the east and west: Russia and Sweden. Hundreds of thousands of Finns died in the crossfire or simply gave up and left.

STRONG FOUNDATIONS FOR THE FUTURE

With the many challenges the Finns have faced, it is time to take another look, but this time forward. Forecasting Finland's future may be a bit easier than it might be for other nations, but it is still a very inexact science. Many important ingredients are in place that allow for better speculation based on the country's assets. First among the assets are the Finnish people themselves. The Finns love their country and take incredible pride in their achievements. Thus, the Finns are the true heart and soul of the country; their amazing perseverance and unflinching ability to rebound from adversity will be the foundation for Finland's future.

The people also provide other key assets for Finland. With a literacy rate of 100 percent and other educational attainment, Finns are some of the world's best-educated people. They are talented, no-nonsense, and honest. In addition, they are one of the world leaders in terms of understanding and using modern computers and communications technology. Access and knowledge of the Internet is amazingly high, and Finns are now consulting around the world with other countries as they share their technical expertise and know-how.

Finland has been consistently recognized as having one of the most successful education systems in the world. Some reasons for this success are Finland's investment in higher education, dedication to training in information technology, and a conscious effort to have highly trained teachers throughout the country's school system.

The country's stable government is another valuable asset. Finland is a strong and proud democracy where women share actively in the power. The parliament alone has more than a century of history, and the new constitution has prepared the Finns for the challenges of the twenty-first century. The importance of the high number of women who govern Finland cannot be overstated. For example, in the 2007 elections, women assumed 12 of the 20 cabinet posts—60 percent—

a figure higher than any other country in the world. Ministries headed by women in 2007 include Agriculture, Transportation, Health, Labor, Justice, Education, Environment, Telecommunications, European Affairs and Immigration, Interior, and Municipal Affairs. In addition, for most of the first decade of the twenty-first century, the Finns had a woman as president. As stated by former Chinese leader Mao Zedong, "Women hold up half the sky," and the women of Finland now lead the world in the implementation of Mao's belief.

The country's political stability also makes it an economic haven, as governmental policies have allowed the country to become one of the world's least corrupt nations. The government is also very protective of legal and property rights, with strong laws to safeguard intellectual property. This is a vital element in protecting the country's high-tech economic interests. Finland's high commitment to freedom of expression and the press also allows for economic development as information flows freely. These and other factors have allowed Finland to be ranked as the second most competitive country in the world, according to the World Economic Forum. All of these elements are promising assets for Finland's economic and political future.

Another vital asset that evolved positively in the last decades of the twentieth century is Finland's relationships with its neighbors. Sweden has not been a threat for well over a century, but Russia and the Soviet Union were a major threat for much of the twentieth century. Political changes in Russia have softened the Finns' mistrust, but it has not totally disappeared. The looming presence of Russia on the eastern frontier is less of a concern today, but Finns have a long memory. Finland's active membership in the European Union is another asset that helps to balance any misdirected intentions that could come in the future from intrusive neighbors. This leaves the Finns with perhaps the best relations that they have had with their next-door neighbors in their history, another good sign for the future.

Other strengths that have emerged are the commercial and scientific advances being made by Finns. As noted earlier, Nokia has evolved from toilet paper to telecommunications, and today is a global leader. Other Finnish companies are also on the cutting edge of new developments in science and business. As an example, a Finn at the University of Helsinki named Linus Torvalds initiated the Linux operating system, a free software competitor to Microsoft Windows, in 1991. As nanotechnology efforts advance, the Finns are well positioned to be among the world's leaders. All of this scientific and technological know-how is planting seeds for the economy of the next generation of Finns.

Other areas also exist as economic strengths that help diversify the economy. Traditional paper pulp and forestry products are still important, but recent growth in industries such as tourism also help to add to the country's financial foundations. As ecotourism grows, Finland is well suited as travelers seek new adventures in places like Lapland. Other tourists from places ranging from Russia to China and India also are increasing at a quality rate that is very promising.

CHALLENGES AHEAD

With all of the assets listed, the country has excellent foundations for a strong future politically, economically, and socially. Some challenges, however, do face the Finns. They range from climate change to social problems like high unemployment, high labor costs, alcoholism, and suicide. The country is working to address these and other issues in a variety of ways. For example, the issue of alcoholism is being addressed by opening liquor stores later, cracking down on Internet alcohol sales, and efforts to reduce binge drinking.

The Finns, whose government believes that carbon-based fuels are a major contributor, are also addressing the larger issue of climate change. Thus, there are important efforts to expand the development and use of nuclear and wind power, as well as new developments in biofuels made from wood

Many European countries are taking action against climate change. To limit the growth of traffic in urban areas, Finns are encouraged to use public transportation and pedestrian and cycling facilities. In addition, low-noise, electrified railcars have been developed to reduce noise pollution, greenhouse gas emissions, and energy consumption.

byproducts. Peat is also used in generating power in some communities as Finnish ingenuity turns to other alternative fuels. Even though nuclear power is used in the country, controversy still exists when new plants are considered. Energy development is crucial to the continuing advancement of Finland's economy. Expectations are high that safe and clean alternatives will be developed to keep economic growth strong, yet without negative impact on the environment. The Green League was included in the ruling coalition in 2007, and the political party has a primary goal of significantly reducing Finland's carbon emissions. Since the Green League in Finland was a fringe party for much of their history, voters have changed and are now seeing their environmental agenda as being very important, as the party has steadily increased its vote tallies. Many of the issues originally raised by the Green League are becoming mainstream concerns, especially the issue of climate change.

FINLAND'S VIRTUAL CENTRALITY

As we finish our Finnish tale, the country and its people seem destined for a very dynamic and prosperous future. The character of the fantastic Finns serves as the core of this optimism, and their determination has carried them very far already. For a country that was once a remote outpost of humankind straddling the Arctic Circle, Finland has now become a twenty-first-century telecommunications superpower. Even though its land was relatively isolated compared to other countries, Finland has transformed itself by the use of technology into a place of virtual centrality. Modern and efficient transportation and communications systems connect Finns to the rest of the world. As a leader in telecommunications, the Finns have virtually relocated themselves to the center of today's global economy and the information age. This is an amazing achievement for a secluded Baltic country with just over 5 million people. Is there much doubt that they will address the challenges of the future efficiently and effectively? Most are betting that, in the end, the resilient and resolute Finns will rise again like the phoenix and succeed, as they always have.

Physical Geography

Location	Northern Europe, bordering the Baltic Sea, Gulf of Bothnia, and Gulf of Finland, between Sweden and Russia with Norway to the north
Area	130,559 square miles (338,145 square kilometers)
Land Features	Mainly low, flat to rolling plains interspersed with lakes and low hills
Climate	Cold temperate; potentially subarctic but comparatively mild because of moderating influence of the surrounding seas and thousands of lakes
Coastline	777 miles (1,250 kilometers)
Land Use	Arable land: 6.54%; permanent crops: 0.02%; other: 93.44%
Natural Hazards	Climate change
Natural Resources	Timber, iron ore, copper, lead, zinc, chromite, nickel, gold, silver, limestone
Environmental Issues	Air pollution from manufacturing and power plants contributing to acid rain; water pollution from industrial wastes, agricultural chemicals; habitat loss threatens wildlife populations

People

Population	5,238,460 (July 2007 est.)
Population Growth Rate	0.127%
Total Fertility Rate	1.73 children born per woman (2007 est.)
Birth Rate	10.42 births per 1,000 population (2007 est.)
Death Rate	9.93 deaths per 1,000 population (2007 est.)
Life Expectancy at Birth	Total population: 78.66 years; male, 75.15 years; female, 82.31 years (2007 est.)
Median Age	Total: 41.6; male, 40; female, 43.1 (2007 est.)
Ethnic Groups	Finn, 93.4%; Swede, 5.7%; Russian, 0.4%; Estonian, 0.2%; Roma (Gypsy), 0.2%; Sami, 0.1%
Religion	Lutheran Church of Finland, 82.5%; Orthodox Church, 1.1%; other Christian, 1.1%; other, 0.1%; unspecified or none, 15.1% (2006)
Languages	Finnish, 92% (official); Swedish, 5.6% (official); other, 2.4% small Sami- and Russian-speaking minorities
Literacy	(Age 15 and over can read and write) Total population: 100% (2000 est.)

Economy

Currency	Euro (Markka prior to 2002)
GDP Purchasing Power Parity (PPP)	$175.2 billion (2006 est.)
GDP Per Capita	$33,500 (2006 est.)
Labor Force	2.65 million
Unemployment	7% of total population (2006 est.)
Labor Force by Occupation	Agriculture and forestry, 4.4%; industry, 17.5%; construction, 6%; commerce, 22%; finance, insurance, and business services, 12%; transport and communications, 8%; public services, 30.2%
Agricultural Products	Barley, wheat, sugar beets, potatoes, dairy cattle, fish
Industries	Metals and metal products, electronics, machinery and scientific instruments, shipbuilding, pulp and paper, foodstuffs, chemicals, textiles, clothing
Exports	$77.52 billion (2006 est.)
Imports	$66.1 billion (2006 est.)
Leading Trade Partners	Exports: Germany, 11.3%; Sweden, 10.5%; Russia, 10.1%; U.K., 6.5%; U.S., 6.5%; Netherlands, 5.1% (2006). Imports: Germany, 15.6%; Russia, 14%; Sweden, 13.7%; Netherlands, 6.6%; China, 5.4%; U.K., 4.7%; Denmark, 4.5% (2006)
Exports Commodities	Machinery and equipment, electronics, chemicals, metals, timber, paper, pulp
Import Commodities	Foodstuffs, petroleum and petroleum products, chemicals, transport equipment, iron and steel, machinery, textile yarn and fabrics, grains
Transportation	Roadways: 48,584 miles (78,189 kilometers), 31,461 miles (50,631 km) paved, including 434 miles (700 km) of expressway; railways: 3,567 miles (5,741 kilometers), 1,627 miles (2,619 km) electrified; airports: 76 with paved runways, 72 with unpaved runways; waterways: 4,872 miles (7,842 km), including Saimaa Canal system of 2,222 miles (3,577 km); southern part leased from Russia
Ports and terminals	Hamina, Hanko, Helsinki, Kotka, Naantali, Pori, Porvoo, Raahe, Rauma, Turku

Government

Country Name Conventional long form: Republic of Finland; conventional short form: Finland; local long form: Suomen tasavalta/Republiken Finland; local short form: Suomi/Finland

Capital Helsinki

Type of Government Republic

Head of Government Prime Minister Matti Vanhanen (since June 24, 2003)

Independence December 6, 1917 (from Russia)

Administrative Divisions Six provinces: Aland, Etela-Suomen Laani, Ita-Suomen Laani, Lansi-Suomen Laani, Lappi, Oulun Laani

Communications

TV Stations 120 (1999 est.)

Radio Stations 189 (AM, 2; FM 186; 1 shortwave)

Phones 7.59 million (including 5.67 million cell phones) (2006 est.)

Internet Users 2.925 million (2006 est.)

*Source: *CIA–The World Factbook* (2007)

100,000+ B.C.	Early people living in Finland around Wolf Cave near Kristinestad.
8,000 B.C.	People living in the area around Antrea, Karelia.
5,000 B.C.	Climate in Finland begins to warm up, a factor encouraging settlement.
4,000 B.C.	People begin to move into Finland from central Russia.
3,000+ B.C.	Baltic people begin to move into Finland.
2,300 B.C.	Agriculture introduced into Finland.
1,500 B.C.	Bronze Age introduced to Finland from Russia.
500 B.C.	Iron Age begins in Finland.
A.D. 98	The Roman historian Tacitus writes about Fenni tribe in the far north of Europe.
First Millenium A.D.	Tribes in southern Finland begin trading with the Vikings from Sweden and Estonia.
1054	Great Schism starts; Finland is located between the two factions.
1155	Swedish King Erik IX orders Bishop Henry, an Englishman, to accompany him on a Roman Catholic Christian crusade to Finland.
1156	Bishop Henry is killed.
1240	First Swedish crusade into eastern Finland fails and is turned back by the Russians.
1242	Second Swedish crusade into eastern Finland fails and is turned back again by the Russians.
1293	Third Swedish crusade into Karelia (eastern Finland) fails and is turned back by the Russians. This crusade resulted in the peace treaty of Pähkinäsaari, signed in 1323.
1300	Turku Cathedral is completed.
1387	Queen Margaret I of Denmark gains control of Norway.
1388	Queen Margaret I is elected as the Swedish sovereign.
1389	King Albert fails in his attempt to retake the Swedish throne by force.

1412	Queen Margaret dies but was responsible for the Kalmar Union, which lasted until 1523.
1475	Olavinlinna Castle constructed on an island in the city of Savonlinna.
1510	Mikael Agricola, a Finn, studies with Martin Luther in Germany.
1517	Martin Luther publishes his *Ninety-five Theses on the Power and Efficacy of Indulgences.*
1523	Gustav Vasa elected king of Sweden.
1527	King Gustav embraces the reform movement of Luther in 1527, adopts the Lutheran faith, and seizes property of the Catholic Church.
1543	Mikael Agricola produced the first Finnish grammar book.
1548	Mikael Agricola first translates the New Testament of the Bible into the Finnish language.
1570	Russo-Swedish War begins.
1595	Russo-Swedish War ends with the Treaty of Tyavzino and with Russia gaining land.
1618	The Thirty Years War begins between Sweden, other countries, and the Habsburg Empire.
1648	The Thirty Years War ends with the Peace of Westphalia and with Sweden recognized as being a major power.
1696	A devastating famine starves one-third of the Finnish population to death.
1700	Great Northern War begins between the Swedish Empire and Poland, Denmark, and Russia.
1714–1722	Russians occupy Finland during the Great Northern War and the Finns suffer greatly.
1721	Great Northern War ends with the Peace of Uusikaupunki, and Finnish lands under the Swedes are lost to the Russians.
1741	Russo-Swedish War begins as Sweden seeks to regain lands lost to Russia in the Great Northern War.
1743	Sweden loses the Russo-Swedish War and also loses more Finnish lands.

1788–1790	Another Russo-Swedish War with the Swedish seeking to regain lands lost in earlier wars. Finnish officers rebel in what is referred to as the Anjala League. This mutiny is viewed today as being an early step toward Finnish independence.
1808	The Finnish War begins and is the final saga in the series of conflicts between the Swedes and Russians.
1809	Russia overruns Finland; the Treaty of Hamina ends the Finnish War, grants Finland to Russia, and ends the 650 years of Swedes' rule over Finland; and the Grand Duchy of Finland is established under Russian rule.
1812	Russians move Finland's capital to Helsinki.
1828	Finland's only university is transferred to Helsinki from Turku.
1865	Nokia company starts as a pulp mill.
1899	Russian tsar Nicholas II issues the February Manifesto, which extends Russian rule in Finland and makes it a province.
1901	Russia usurps the Finnish Army and conscripts Finns as soldiers.
1906	Finland forms a unicameral parliament called the Eduskunta; universal suffrage gives Finnish women the right to vote; Finland is only the second European nation to grant this right to women.
1917	Russian Revolution breaks out and weakens Russian grip on Finland; Grand Duchy of Finland ends, and Finland becomes independent.
1919	Finland adopts a new constitution.
1920	Finland joins the League of Nations; Treaty of Dorpat signed between Finland and Russia.
1932	Ten-year nonaggression pact signed between Russia and Finland.
1939	Germany and Soviet Union sign the Nazi-Soviet Non-Aggression Pact; Soviet Union attacks Finland on November 30; F.E. Sillanpää wins the Nobel Prize for literature.

1940 After the Winter War, Finland is forced to give up a part of Karelia to the Soviets in the Treaty of Moscow; German-Finnish Agreement signed as the Finns try to hedge against the Soviet Union.

1941 Germany attacks the Soviet Union, and the Soviets attack Finland.

1944 Finns lose the second war, called the Continuation War, with the Soviet Union.

1945 Finland wins the Lapland War with Germany.

1948 Treaty of Friendship, Cooperation, and Mutual Assistance is signed between Finland and the Soviet Union (also renewed in 1955, 1970, and 1983).

1952 Summer Olympic Games are held in Helsinki.

1955 Finland joins the United Nations.

1986 Finland joins the European Free Trade Association.

1989 Finland joins the Council of Europe.

1991 Linus Torvalds at the University of Helsinki initiates the Linux operating system.

1992 Treaty of Friendship, Cooperation, and Mutual Assistance is declared null and void by Russia and Finland.

1995 Finland joins the European Union.

2000 Finland adopts a new constitution, the first since the 1919 constitution; Tarja Halonen is elected the first woman president of Finland; Turku Cathedral celebrates its seven-hundredth anniversary.

2005 Nokia's mobile phone sales total nearly one billion.

2006 The Eduskunta celebrates its one-hundredth year of existence as Finland's legislative body and also marks the one-hundredth anniversary of women in Finland having the right to vote; Tarja Halonen is reelected as president of Finland; Finland's Eduskunta ratifies the EU Constitution.

2007 Elections held for Eduskunta which creates a new, more conservative, coalition consisting of the National Coalition Party, Center Party, Green League, and the Swedish People's Party; Finnish women head 60 percent of the country's ministries, which is the highest percentage in the world.

Bibliography

Brewer, Jennifer, and Markus Lehtipuu. *Lonely Planet Finland*. Oakland: Lonely Planet, 1999.

Lee, Phil, Lone Mouritsen, James Procter, and Neil Roland. *The Rough Guide to Scandinavia, 5th ed.* London: Rough Guides, 2003.

Ross, Zoe, ed. *Insight Guide Finland*. Insight Guides. Maspeth, N.Y.: Langenscheidt, 2003.

Singleton, Fred. *A Short History of Finland*. Cambridge: Cambridge University Press, 1998.

Swallow, Deborah. *Culture Shock! Finland: A Guide to Customs and Etiquette*. Portland: Graphic Arts Center, 2001.

Engman, Max, and David Kirby, eds. *Finland: People, Nation, State.* London: C. Hurst, 1989.

Haikio, Martti. *A Brief History of Modern Finland.* Helsinki: University of Helsinki, 1992.

Jakobson, Max. *Finland in the New Europe.* London: Praeger, 1998.

Jowett, Philip. *Finland at War 1939–1945.* New York: Osprey, 2006.

Jutikkala, Eino, and Kauko Pirinen. *A History of Finland.* New York: Dorset Press, 1989.

Kirby, David. *A Concise History of Finland.* Cambridge Concise Histories. Cambridge: Cambridge University Press, 2006.

Lavery, Jason. *The History of Finland.* Westport, Conn.: Greenwood Press, 2006.

Leney, Terttu. *Finland—Culture Smart: A Quick Guide to Customs and Etiquette.* London: Kuperard, 2006.

Lewis, Richard D. *Finland, Cultural Lone Wolf.* Yarmouth, Maine: Intercultual Press, 2004.

Web Sites

About.com
http://geography.about.com/library/maps/blfinland.htm
This site provides geographic perspectives on Finland.

Center for the Study of Global Change
http://webdb.iu.edu/internationalprograms/scripts/accesscoverpage.cfm?country=Finland
Indiana University site with extensive information and links to other sites on Finland.

City of Helsinki
http://www.hel.fi/wps/portal/Helsinki_en/?WCM_GLOBAL_CONTEXT=/en/Helsinki/
Web site of the city of Helsinki with links to information on education and culture in the capital.

Countries and Their Cultures
http://www.everyculture.com/Cr-Ga/Finland.html
Extensive cultural report on Finland.

Country Reports

http://www.countryreports.org/country.aspx?countryid=82&countryName=Finland

This site provides information on Finland and other countries of the world.

Finland Government Sites

http://www.worldwide-tax.com/finland/fingov.asp

Web site with links to various Finnish government agencies and bodies.

Finnish Embassy in the United States

http://www.finland.org/en/

Official site of Finland's embassy in the United States with extensive information on the country.

Finnish Tourist Board

http://www.visitfinland.com/w5/index.nsf/(pages)/index

Finland's official tourism Web site with information on the geography of Finland and travel in the country.

iExplore

http://www.iexplore.com/dmap/Finland/Overview

Site provides information on Finland's history and culture with links to sites on city information.

Index Mundi

http://www.indexmundi.com/finland/index.html#Government

Extensive site with information on Finland's geography, history, economics, and many other areas.

International Constitutional Law (ICL)

http://www.servat.unibe.ch/law/icl/fi00000_.html

Contains text of Finland's constitution.

London's Global University

http://www.ssees.ac.uk/finland.htm

Provides a guide to key Internet resources on Finland and other countries.

Lonely Planet World Guide

http://www.lonelyplanet.com/worldguide/destinations/europe/finland/

Travel guide's Web site with information on travel, pictures, events, history and culture in Finland.

Maps of World

http://mapsofworld.com/finland/

This site provides a variety of maps of Finland and other locations.

One World Nations Online
http://www.nationsonline.org/oneworld/
Extensive site with links to other sites on Finland.

Population Reference Bureau
http://www.prb.org/Countries/Finland.aspx
Site provides detailed population statistics for Finland and other countries.

President of Finland
http://www.president.fi/en/
The official Web site of the president of Finland.

Statistics Finland
http://www.stat.fi/tup/suoluk/suoluk_alue_en.html
Site provides an array of statistical information on Finland from mostly government research.

U.S. Department of State: Background Notes
http://www.state.gov/r/pa/ei/bgn/3238.htm
Provides an extensive overview of Finland's history, economy, government, and many other areas.

U.S. Library of Congress
http://lcweb2.loc.gov/frd/cs/fitoc.html
This site provides extensive history, geography, economic, and other perspectives of Finland and other world countries.

Virtual Finland
http://virtual.finland.fi/
Extensive Finnish site with information on the country's history, geography, economy, culture, and a wide variety of other information.

Wikipedia
http://en.wikipedia.org/wiki/Finland
This is an online encyclopedia that presents extensive information on Finland and other countries of the world.

The World Factbook
https://cia.gov/cia//publications/factbook/geos/fi.html
This Central Intelligence Agency (CIA) site provides up-to-date information about Finland and other nations of the world.

Picture Credits

Index

Index

DOUGLAS A. PHILLIPS is a lifetime educator, writer, and consultant who has worked in and traveled to more than 100 countries on 6 continents. In 2006, he was admitted to the Traveler's Century Club based in California. During his career, he has been a middle-school teacher, curriculum developer, author, and trainer of educators in numerous countries around the world. Phillips has served as the president of the National Council for Geographic Education, and he has received the Outstanding Service Award from the National Council for the Social Studies, along with many other awards. Phillips lives in Arizona with his family, where he writes and serves as an educational consultant for the Center for Civic Education.

CHARLES F. GRITZNER is Distinguished Professor of Geography at South Dakota State University in Brookings. He is now in his fifth decade of college teaching and research. In addition to classroom instruction, he enjoys travel, writing, working with teachers, and sharing his love of geography with readers. As a senior consulting editor for Chelsea House Publishers' *Modern World Nations* and *Major World Cultures* series, he has a wonderful opportunity to combine each of these "hobbies." Dr. Gritzner has served as both president and executive director of the National Council for Geographic Education and has received the council's highest honor, the George J. Miller Award for Distinguished Service to Geographic Education, as well as other honors from the NCGE, Association of American Geographers, and other organizations.